Three Mile Harbor

East Hampton's Priceless Gem
— A Pictorial History—

By Sylvia Mendelman

Seacoast Publishing, East Hampton, New York

Three Mile Harbor

East Hampton's Priceless Gem
—A Pictorial History—

by Sylvia Mendelman

Published by Seacoast Publishing
423 Three Mile Harbor HC Road
East Hampton, New York 11937

Email: seacoastpublishing@hamptons.com

Art Direction and Graphic Design by Diane C. Hewett.
Editor/Copy Editor, Elizabeth A. Torjussen

Printed by The Museum Press, New York, NY.
Printed in China.

Library of Congress Control Number: 2001116264
Mendelman, Sylvia, 1936-
Three Mile Harbor—East Hampton's Priceless Gem/A Pictorial History
includes bibliographical references,
interview list and index

ISBN 0-9703368-0-2

1. East Hampton (N.Y.) - History
2. East Hampton (N.Y.) - History - Pictorial works
974.7'25-dc21
CIP

This history of Three Mile Harbor has been prepared to be as accurate as possible given the resources
available to the author. The author will not be held responsible for inaccuracies in the text.

Previous page: Aerial view of Three Mile Harbor looking north. (Aerial photograph by James T. Abts, Hamilton, Massachusetts, 2002)

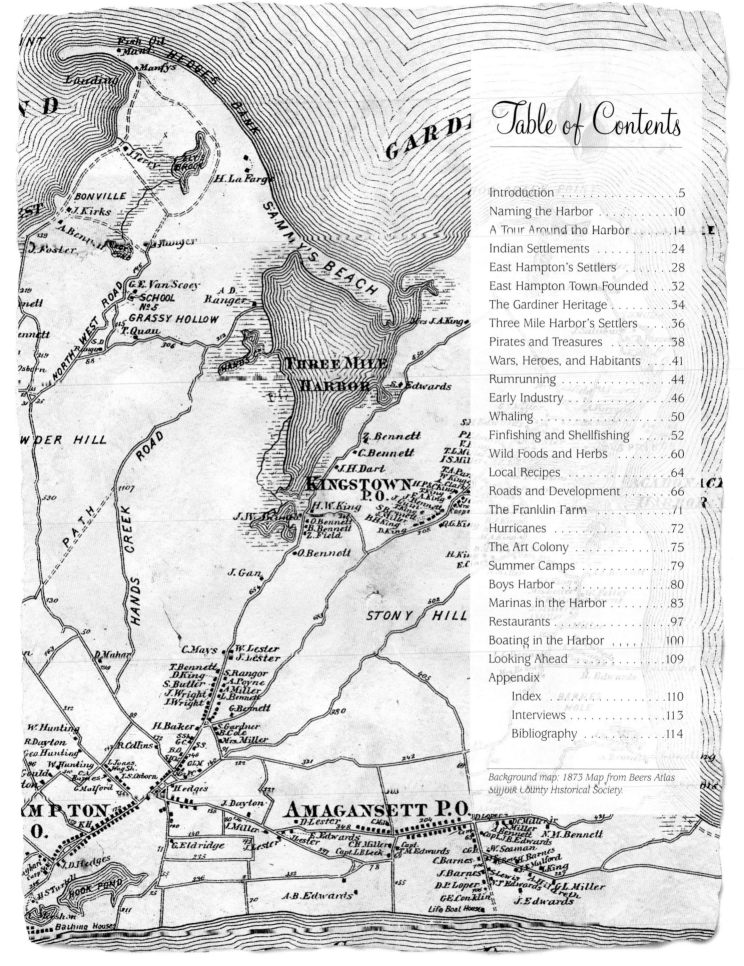

Table of Contents

Background map: 1873 Map from Beers Atlas Suffolk County Historical Society.

Above: Dusk in Three Mile Harbor
(Photo © 2001 by Gordon M. Grant)
Right: "Moonlight on Three
Mile Harbor" (Postcard from the
Harvey Ginsberg Collection at
East Hampton Library)
Facing Page
Top: "Sudden Squall" at Maidstone
Jetty (Oil on canvas by Carl Scorza)
Middle: Sailboarding with a stiff
breeze off Maidstone Park (Photo
by Diane C. Hewett)
Bottom: Pound trap hauling demon-
stration by Bill Schultz for "A Day In
Springs," celebrating East Hampton
Town's 350th anniversary, September
11, 1998 (Photo by Diane C. Hewett)

Moonlight on Three Mile Harbor, L.I.

Introduction

T hree Mile Harbor, a radiant blue sapphire shining from the crown worn on elegant East Hampton's head … a rocking cradle for the boats anchored in its care … an azure treasure chest filled with clams, scallops, oysters, eels, whelks, crabs, and fishermen's dreams … this is East Hampton's priceless gem called Three Mile Harbor.

The sea's bounty rushes through the jagged jetty at the mouth of the Harbor with each tide's flow. Rushing waters tilt channel buoys until the tide runs slack. Waters in the coves and sheltered marinas are calm and safe havens for newly spawned sea life. Shorebirds feast on the shellfish and shiners in the grasses and seaweed. Freshwater springs along the shore attract animals and wildlife such as foxes, deer, raccoons, opossums, muskrats, mice, frogs, and turtles. The springs provide a freshwater supply year-round.

Three Mile Harbor's waters are enjoyable every season of the year, but the summer's outdoor activity attracts the most people. Fishermen, clammers, water-skiers, boaters, swimmers, and hikers are drawn to these pristine waters. Boaters can dock at marinas or moor in a designated area. Two popular swimming spots — Maidstone Park and Sammy's Beach — are just outside the Harbor on the shores of Gardiner's Bay. Sometimes a boat's wake travels to shore, making waves that delight the children bobbing in their tubes. Water-skiers have a specially reserved area in the northwestern corner inside

The Maidstone Park peninsula's mile-long loop — flanked by beach plums, bayberry, wild roses, asters, and other wildflowers — is a beautiful place to walk or run by the water. Ospreys, sea gulls, terns, and a variety of songbirds fly overhead, providing some "country music."

The pavilion by the jetty is a popular spot for picnic suppers or a barbeque while watching a variety of boats come and go into the Harbor. The eastern end of Maidstone Park has a ball field, popular with both Little League and adult teams.

The many restaurants along the eastern shore of the Harbor are crowded on summer evenings with diners enjoying excellent food and fantastic sunsets.

Any time of day or night, the Harbor offers a glorious experience for those lucky enough to be here. One night, my husband dragged me out of bed at 4 A.M. to see the moon, bright and full, a huge shimmering ball setting in the west, casting a reflection in the water. Memorable!

the Harbor and in Gardiner's Bay, along Sammy's Beach. Sailboards arrive when the wind is right. Fishermen of all ages try casting from the shores, especially near the jetty. Clammers can be seen waist-deep, digging with their rakes and storing their catch in tubes fitted with baskets.

Left: *Winter of 1956 — taken at the Head of the Harbor. Huckleberry, the pony, is pulling a sleigh with Harvey Field and the Dave Edwards' family. The sleigh was built by the James E. Gay Blacksmith Shop for William Hubbard King of Springs. (Photo from the Patricia A. Field family collection)*
Right: *Winter at Sammy's Beach (Acrylic on canvas by Scott Hewett)*

Fall's cooler water and stronger winds change the Harbor's pace and scenery. Brisk winds challenge sailboats, filling their sails and driving their hulls through the waves as though plowing a field.

Hauling boats out and storing them away for the winter begins in the fall, but fishermen eager to catch the "big ones" keep their boats in the water through the fall. Migrating fish are the talk of sport and commercial fishermen dreaming of bountiful catches of blues and striped bass. Where's the best spot? Watch the birds! They hover and dive for the bait fish in the water. Then again, a true fisherman never tells anyone where the "really good spot" is. Scallop season also opens in the fall, and the anticipation of a "good season" creates excitement among the "scallopers" to find this treasure in the Harbor. Scallops don't stay in one spot the way clams do, so finding them among the seaweed and rocks can be frustrating. The catch can be very scarce, and many give up after one day.

Leaves on the trees fringing the edges of the Harbor change from verdant green to orange, crimson, and yellow. Incredible shades of blue are shared between the sky and water. Storms and winds whip up whitecaps on the tips of waves like the meringue on a pie. "Nor'easters" can be incredibly fierce in Gardiner's Bay just outside the Harbor's protection. A so-called Nor'easter, the hurricane of 1938, sank the fishing boat *Gertrude* as the fishermen were trying to pull in their nets.

Winters can be very cold. When the ice is thick, eelers try their luck through holes cut in the ice, and ice-boaters skim over the frozen waters. Huge chunks of ice float in and out with the tides, wreaking havoc on bulkheads and docks. The winters of 1934 and 1970–71 were so cold that the Harbor and Gardiner's Bay froze thick enough for a truck to drive out to Gardiner's Island!

Winter views of the Harbor are framed by stark woodlands along the shoreline. Pumpkin-colored skies are etched with silhouettes of branches in the early evening. On cold mornings, the water is a dark sapphire blue or ominous gray, mirroring the sky above. When winds lash the waves in Gardiner's Bay, locals say, *"whitecaps 'r big in th' bay, Bub!"*

Springtime's warmth awakens the fluke and flounder buried in the mud on the Harbor's bottom. Fishermen position their boats in the channel and try their luck. There's nothing better than the taste of the sweet, fresh fish of spring. Boatyards prepare the boats that were blocked up for the winter. Covers are removed, bottoms are painted, topsides cleaned, and then they are launched. A spring cleaning of vacation homes also begins, gardens are tended, and another "season" has begun.

In spring, sunsets move from the southwestern sky to the west in spectacular displays of peach, mauve, crimson, and ochre. Tiny chartreuse leaves bud out on trees along the shore. Flowering beach plum, lilac, pear, and cherry blossoms scent the air. Lupines, violets, and other wildflowers scatter themselves in undisturbed spots. Rare wildflowers, like lady's-slippers, are still found in undisturbed woodland.

Birds return to nest once more. The first to return is the osprey, nesting on its high-poled platform. Eagles have also been sighted recently. Red-winged blackbirds, robins, orioles, bluebirds, mockingbirds, and others join those that stayed here in the winter. The warmth of the earth wakes turtles, snakes, salamanders, insects, and all sorts of wildlife eager to enjoy the outdoors once more.

Charles Towne said, "Water is to a landscape what eyes are to a human face." Three Mile Harbor, this teardrop from the eye of God, illuminates and mirrors the East Hampton landscape, adding sparkle and beauty to this shoreline.

In 1930, in a speech to the Lions Club of East Hampton, Irwin Cobb called Three Mile Harbor "the front door of East Hampton." It certainly is an impressive entry to this beautiful town! ❧

Photo by Diane C. Hewett

*H*ow did the Harbor get its name? Three Mile Harbor is first recorded in Town Records in 1655. On April 10, 1655, Chief Wyandanch, the Chief Sachem of Paumanock, signed a pact with Rev. Thomas James and the proprietors of East Hampton for a fence to protect pasturage for cattle to go from "the head of the Harbor called three mile harbor to the south side of the Towne of East Hampton, that is to say from sea to sea for the keeping off of horses from going eastward in the summer." Again, Town Records referred to Three Mile Harbor in 1676, but nowhere on record was a reason given for naming it "Three Mile Harbor."

Facing Page: Three Mile Harbor is three miles to East Hampton's Historic Village and also three miles to Amagansett. (Referenced from map courtesy of the Town of East Hampton)
Above: *Three Mile Harbor buoy. (Photo by Edna Renner)*
Below: *Plaque at "Sandy Hook," the intersection of Three Mile Harbor and Springs-Fireplace Road, reads "This land donated to the people of the Town of East Hampton by the East Hampton Lions Club on December 24, 1971."*

Some people mistakenly think that the Harbor is three miles long or wide or even three miles deep. The Harbor is actually 2.3 miles long and 14 feet at its deepest point.

The Town Trustees' Records show that a proposal was made in 1937 to change the name of the Harbor to East Hampton Harbor, but nothing came of the proposal.

In Paul Bailey's *Long Island*, vol.1, published in 1949, Mary E. Bell wrote, "Three Mile Harbor… lies three miles from East Hampton Village". The Head of the Harbor was three miles from the site of the first settlers' meetinghouse, or "Ordinary." The Village flagpole by the pond is now at this site.

The Head of Three Mile Harbor is geographically at the peak of a triangle that forms between East Hampton and Amagansett. The distance from either village to the Harbor is three miles by taking either Three Mile Harbor Road or Abraham's Path. Perhaps "three miles to the harbor" became "Three Mile Harbor" by dropping the little words "to the" over time.

The original road from the village to the Harbor ended at the Head of the Harbor. There was a cow path extending beyond that, but little else. Three Mile Harbor Road began at the intersection of Fireplace Road and Three Mile Harbor Road at an area known as Sandy Hook. House numbering started at Sandy Hook and went up to the Head of the Harbor, where the original road ended. In the 1800s, a dirt road extended north of the Head of the Harbor, called Penny's Highway in honor of Joshua Penny, a hero from the War of 1812. Houses on this northern stretch of Three Mile Harbor Road were numbered starting with one again, causing some duplicate numbers for Three Mile Harbor Road. To eliminate the duplicate-numbering confusion, the northern strip was renamed Three Mile Harbor Road/Hog Creek Highway. A simple name of Three Mile Harbor Road, North and South, might have been a better solution. Currently, people who live on the northern section must address their mail with an excessively long name.

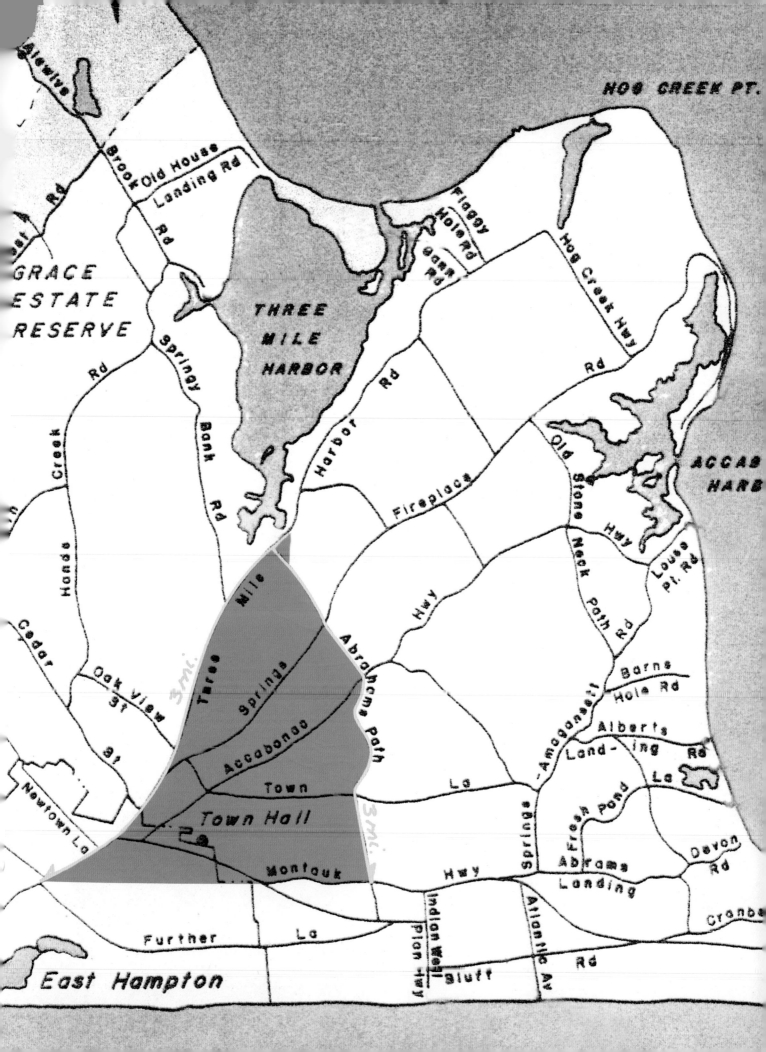

WEST HARBOR

FISH FACTORY
C. 1870'S

SES BANKS

3

OLD WOOD LANDING

SPLIT ROCK

ALEWIFE BRK.

ALEWIFE BROOK POND

J. TERRY HOMESTEAD RUINS C. 1800

CEMETERY 1700-1800'S

2

LAFARGES LANDING

KIRK'S PLACE

ALEWIFE

GARDINERS BAY

SCOY'S POND

NORTH WEST LANDING

CEMETERY 1700-1800'S
Van Scoy Homestead Ruins C.1771

OLD HOUSE LANDING ROAD

4

LUCY'S POINT

SAMMY'S BEACH

1

22

BARNES MEADOWS

SETTLEMENT OF NORTHWEST C. 1663-1770

BUFFALO WALLER HILL

TOBE'S HILL

BAKER'S ISLAND

19

PEN- SEDE ISLAN

GREAT SWAMP

Schoolhouse Ruins C.1792

SINEA'S CORNERS

MULLET HOLLOW

6

ELI CHANNEL

5

NORTH WEST SWAMP

CEMETERY 1800'S

TRYPHENA'S HOLLOW

GOOSE ISLAND

16

18

SQUAW COVE

ELLA LAN'S

POWDER HILL

GRASSY HOLLOW

BROOK

ASHAWAGH INDIAN SETTLEMENT

7

8

PETER'S REEL

THREE MILE HARBOR

17

ROAD

BENNETT CEMETERY

ROAD TO POWDER

HANDS CREEK

DUCK CREEK

15

ATER

JOSHUA'S HOLE

SCOY'S

SCOWWOOD HOLLOW

9

DOMINY'S POINT

BLACK MEADOW

14

ATFIELDS HOLE

NECK

ROAD

LONG HILL

PATH

BASSWOOD

HARBOR

13

COBBLER'S HILL

OLD NORTH WEST ROAD

CREEK

INDIAN CAMP

CEDAR POND

12

COPECES

SPRINGY BANKS

10

LONG BEACH

MILE

JASON'S ROCK

HANDS

PATH

HEDGES CREEK

SNAKE HOLE

FRESH MEADOW

SHADOM

HARD SCRABBLE

ROUND SWAMP

THREE

11

27

(Abraham's Path)

FIREPLACE

ROAD

KI

NORTH

WHALEBONE

SOAKHIDE CREEN

TWO HOLES OF WATER

LO

WEST

NEW GROUND

28

PLAINS

D. Lester T. Lester

SPRINGS

STONY

EAST HAMPTON

29

FREETOWN

ACCABONAC

AMAGA

31

30

Settled in

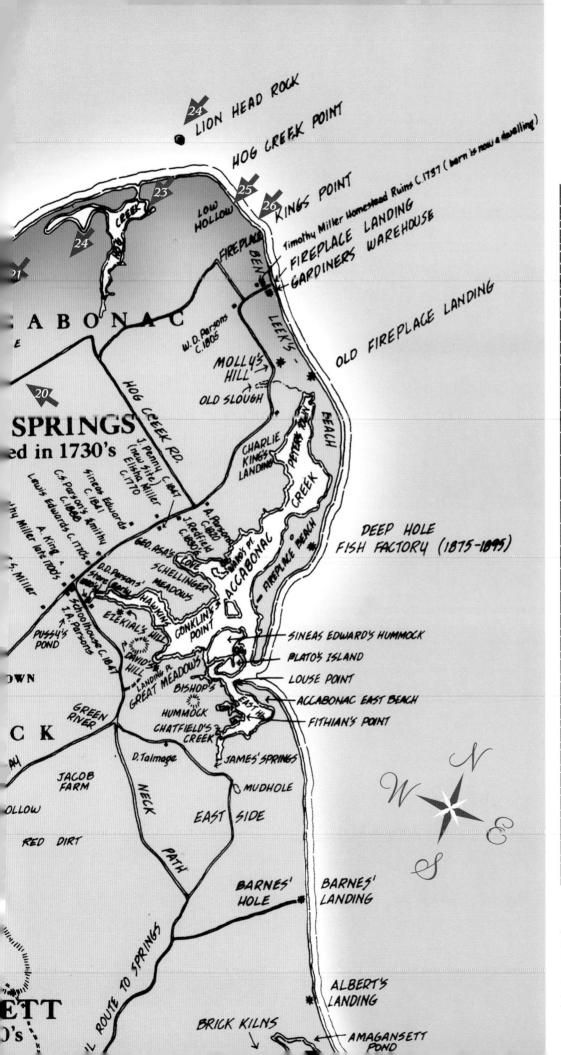

LION HEAD ROCK

HOG CREEK POINT

24

25 KINGS POINT

26

LOW HOLLOW

23

Timothy Miller Homestead Ruins C.1757 (barn is now a dwelling)

FIREPLACE LANDING

GARDINERS WAREHOUSE

FIREPLACE

BEN

CREEK

21

A B O N A C

W. D. Parsons C.1805

LEEK'S

OLD FIREPLACE LANDING

MOLLY'S HILL

OLD SLOUGH

20

HOG CREEK RD.

J. Penny C. 1847 (new Site) Elisha Miller C.1770

CHARLIE KING'S LANDING

PETER TOWN

BEACH

SPRINGS

ed in 1730's

Sineas Edwards C. 1841

C.S. Parson's Smithy C. 1888

Lewis Edwards C. 1880

A. Parsons C.1820

J. Redfield C. 1800

A. King

ACCABONAC

DEEP HOLE FISH FACTORY (1875-1895)

thy Miller late 1800s

GEO. ASA'S

LOVE

SPADY'S PT.

CREEK

FIREPLACE BEACH

S. Miller

D.D. Parsons'

SCHELLINGER

MEADOWS

Stone Betty

HAWKINS

School house C. 1847

J.A. Parsons

EZEKIAL'S HILL

CONKLIN'S POINT

SINEAS EDWARD'S HUMMOCK

PUSSY'S POND

R. DAVID'S HILL

Landing Pl. GREAT MEADOWS

BISHOP'S

EAST H.

PLATO'S ISLAND

LOUSE POINT

ACCABONAC EAST BEACH

OWN

GREEN RIVER

HUMMOCK

CHATFIELD'S CREEK

FITHIAN'S POINT

C K

D. Talmage

JAMES' SPRINGS

AY

JACOB FARM

NECK

MUDHOLE

OLLOW

EAST SIDE

RED DIRT

PATH

N

W E

S

BARNES' HOLE

BARNES' LANDING

L ROUTE TO SPRINGS

ETT

0's

BRICK KILNS

ALBERT'S LANDING

AMAGANSETT POND

Key

Descriptions of locations are on the following pages.

1 Sammy's Beach
2 LaFarges Landing
3 Hedges Banks
4 Lucy's Point
5 Eli Channel
6 Mullet Hollow
7 Peter's Reel
8 Hands Creek
9 Dominy's Point
10 Springy Banks
11 Soak Hides Road
12 Copeces Lane
13 Will Curl Highway
14 Shagwong
15 Duck Creek
16 Keyes' Island
17 Gardiner Avenue
18 Gann Road
19 Penny Sedge Island
20 Flaggy Hole Road
21 Blue Bay Girl Scout Camp
22 Maidstone Park
23 Hog Creek
24 Lion Head
25 Low Hollow
26 Kings Point
27 Abraham's Path
28 Round Swamp
29 Freetown
30 Neighborhood House
31 Sandy Hook

Map illustration — 1976 East Hampton Town Historical Map by Thomas M. Thoroon and Norton W. Daniels, colorized by Diane C. Hewett. (Please note, arrows indicate general locations.)

A Tour Around the Harbor

Street names and localities around the Harbor reflect the history of the area. Some were named after old Indian place names, some after heroes and early inhabitants, some for land use, and some were named by developers. (Place names are keyed to the map on pages 12 and 13.)

Starting on the northwestern shore is **Sammy's Beach (1)**. It is named after one of the many "Samuels" in East Hampton, but no one knows which one. A Samuel Parsons lived in the village in 1655, and Samuel and Robert Parsons bought the peninsula in 1731.

There is a popular story attributing the name Sammy's Beach to Samuel Sherrill, captain of a cargo ship from Connecticut, who ran aground on the beach with "Mulliner" hope chests in the hold, which had been specially made in New Haven for some ladies in East Hampton. Word got to town that the ladies could claim their hope chests at Sammy's Beach. Miss Elizabeth Parsons was among the ladies who went to the beach. She met Samuel Sherrill there and said that he was the most handsome man she had ever seen. They were soon married.

Another Samuel figured in its history in 1839. That year, the peninsula was bought by Samuel, Henry, and Jeremiah Terry from Jonathan Mulford.

In 1890, David J. Gardiner bought the peninsula. He installed a gate north of Hands Creek to keep his cattle from straying. He even tried to raise

bison, but he gave up the project after a few years. The Lester family owned the property after that and eventually sold it to the Town for use as parkland and a nature preserve.

Old House Landing Road provided access to **LaFarges Landing (2)** on Gardiner's Bay, to the west of Sammy's Beach. It was named for Henry LaFarge, who lived there during the 1870s. He bought it from Ebenezer Hedges, whose ancestor, William, originally operated a farm there in the 1700s. The area was a "convenient anchoring ground for outward bound whaling ships," wrote Judge Henry P. Hedges. Sherrill Foster remembers that her uncle would take the cord wood he had chopped from his lot in the Northwest Woods to LaFarges Landing to load it on a ship for delivery to New York City.

Hedges Banks(3) is named after Ebenezer Hedges. His ancestor was William Hedges, who was listed in the 1655 Town Records and lived in East Hampton Village at the southern end of Main Street. Hedges Banks is a high bluff overlooking Gardiners Bay, an excellent vantage point for scanning the horizon for approaching ships.

Lucy's Point (4), as indicated on some old maps, was on the south side of Sammy's Beach and is no longer a "point" of land.

Eli Channel (5), a deepwater channel paralleling the shoreline between Sammy's Beach and Hands Creek, was named after Eli Parsons, who lived there in the early 1800s. This was and still is a favorite spot to get a "mess of clams and scallops."

Above: *"Winter Fog 1999," Three Mile Harbor Jetty, (Oil on canvas by Ralph Carpentier) Hedges Bank is seen in the distance.*

Facing Page

Top: *September 2000 aerial view of the entrance to the Harbor, with Sammy's Beach on the west side of the channel and Maidstone Park on the east side. South of Maidstone Park is Penny Sedge Island, the Harbor Marina, and the Commercial Dock. (Photo by Diane C. Hewett)*

Bottom: *Bison raised by David J. Gardiner on the northwestern shores of the Harbor in 1910 (Photo courtesy of East Hampton Star)*

Federated Eastern Indian League sponsored the Pow Wow with help from Chief Red Cloud, Chief Swimming Eel, and Carlos Tex (Chief Red Thundercloud from the Catawba tribe of South Carolina). During this Pow Wow, the Montauk Indians signed a treaty of peace on deerskin with their historical foes, the Narragansett Indians. This occasion was celebrated with tribal dances and songs, to which the public was invited. The Pow Wows ended when the area was developed and the area's name was changed to Hampton Waters. The road paralleling the Harbor kept the name of Springy Banks.

There are two small ponds with brackish waters in this area: Oyster Pond is at the northern end of Oyster Shores Road and Weir Point Pond is on the southern end.

Soak Hides Road (11), a connecting road between Three Mile Harbor Road and Springy Banks Road, was named for the practice of soaking hides there in the dreen, or stream, to cure them in the acidic, tannin-rich waters. The dreen, called Tanbark, originates just north of Round Swamp and flows northward toward the Harbor, crossing over Three Mile Harbor Road near Springy Banks Road and emptying into the Harbor by Soak Hides Road. There were 44 townspeople employed in the leather industry here in 1778. Many homes along Three Mile Harbor Road had tanning tubs in their yards.

Mullet Hollow (6), a landing place for the local fishermen, was halfway between Sammy's Beach and **Peter's Reel (7),** named for Peter Quaw, who lived there in the 1860s.

Hands Creek (8) and Hands Creek Road are named after John Hand, one of the original settlers. John was the father of Stephen Hand, whose name is on an Indian deed dated 1660. Hand's Creek was the site of an old Indian campground called Ashawagh, meaning "between the forks" (of water).

Dominy's Point (9) is a landing off a wooded lot where the Dominys cut wood for their cabinetry. Records from their account books from 1765 to 1820 record "Carting wood from Harbr Lot" to their shop in East Hampton. W. T. Dominy also kept his large party boat in Three Mile Harbor in the 1920s.

Springy Banks (10), an area on the southwestern shore of the Harbor, is named after the freshwater springs bubbling to the surface by the shores there. Early cisterns were made to collect the water by using a hollowed-out tree trunk. This constant, natural supply of fresh water was important for the horses and cows, as well as for the people settling there. Because there were waters bubbling to the surface around that area, there was an old cistern for public use at the Head of the Harbor. Mary Louise Dodge remembers that it had a tin cup next to it for drinking.

Springy Banks was a favored campground for the Indian tribes' annual "Pow-Wow" starting in the 1930s. In 1944, the Long Island Council of the

Copeces Lane (12), on the southeastern shore of Three Mile Harbor, is named for an Indian word meaning "little cove" or "little place of shelter." It was mentioned in Town Records in 1705, in which a Mr. Miller exchanged "a certain piece of meadow ground lying at or near the head of the Three Mile Harbor at a place called Copeces being by estimation about three acres." The waters at the Head of the Harbor had been enclosed, or "shut in," by a narrow peninsula called Long Beach, stretching out from the eastern shore of Three Mile Harbor, now called Breeze Hill Road. There was a very narrow weir, or channel, on the western end of this peninsula, the only entry into a very sheltered inner harbor, or cove. The Indians beached their canoes on the shore of this cove. In 1931, a cut was made on the eastern end of Long Beach and dredged, facilitating the exit of boats from the newly built Maidstone Boat Club facility.

4980   SCENE AT THREE MILE, HARBOR, L. I.   ILLUSTRATED POST CARD CO., N. Y.

Above: *Postcard from the Harvey Ginsberg Collection at East Hampton Library*

Below: *Fishermen in the shallow waters at the Head of the Harbor hauling their nets into their boat*

Facing Page

Top: *"Split Rock" is thought to be the largest rock in the area. Glacial deposits left it on Founders Lane in Settlers Landing on the west side of the Harbor. Giving some perspective of its size, Sylvia Mendelman stands to the right. Interestingly, there is another huge rock on Crows Nest Lane in the same development.*

Bottom: *Plaque marking Soak Hides Dreen (Tanbark) on Soak Hides Road. Plaque reads:*

SOAK HIDE DREEN
This stream was once used for the softening of hides prior to their being made into leather goods.

Left: "Black Marsh" or "Black Meadow," as photographed by the Grom brothers in the 1950s
(Photos courtesy of C.E. King)
Above: Shagwong Marina (Photo courtesy of Atlantic Cruising Club, Inc.)

Will Curl Highway (13) was named for an Indian who camped under a mulberry tree at the end of that road.

The names of **Shagwong (14)** and **Fort Pond Boulevard** were copycat names of locations in Montauk. These names were given to locations in Springs in the 1920s when there was much real estate development in Montauk by Carl Fisher. The story told is that investors would buy these properties along Three Mile Harbor sight unseen, thinking they were located in Montauk. *Shagwong* means "on the side of a hill" in the Indian language. The site of Shagwong Marina is actually where the old "Black Meadow" or "Marsh" was located, which was subsequently dredged out to develop the marina.

Duck Creek (15) is on the southern loop of Squaw Road, and the Town's Commercial Dock is on its northern end. On this eastern shore, squaws made wampum from an abundant resource of shells. Ilse O'Sullivan mentioned Squaw Cove as an ancient Indian village in her book *The Springs*.

Keyes' Island (Dayton's Island, Wallace Island, or Goose Island) (16), just off the shores of Squaw Road, is privately owned. The story is told that E. T. Dayton was using the 4-acre island for hunting in

the 1920s and had a little shack on it. The shack was gradually enlarged to a house. It was a barebones place, with no water or electricity. He got water by laying a pipe from the mainland, but every now and then a boat's keel would break it. In the late 1960s, Dayton sold it to Charlie Keyes. Charlie's son, Cliff, now enjoys summers on the island, renamed Gull Island. It is a picturesque island and one of the treasures of Three Mile Harbor.

Gardiner Avenue (17) is named for the Gardiner family, settlers of Gardiner's Island. Just south of Gardiner Avenue is one of the oldest houses on Three Mile Harbor Road. It was built in the early eighteenth century for the Bennett family and then bought by A. M. Payne. Francis Gardiner Collins, one of Winthrop Gardiner's daughters, known in East Hampton as "Fanny," bought it and raised horses and other animals there. She remembers that her sister, Isabel, had two debutante coming-out parties. When Winthrop asked Fanny when she wanted her party, she replied, "I'm not going to a party with a 'For Sale' sign on my back!" and rode off on her horse. She loved her horses, especially her black stallion, and often galloped in the fields next to her house. Other animals, such as Priscilla the Pig and a goat named Elvis, became special attractions for children and their families. Fanny's

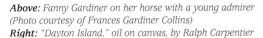

Above: *Fanny Gardiner on her horse with a young admirer (Photo courtesy of Frances Gardiner Collins)*
Right: *"Dayton Island," oil on canvas, by Ralph Carpentier*

daughter, Mary, now owns the property and operates a farmstand there called Pigpen Produce.

Gann Road (18) honors John Gann, a hero of the War of 1812, and also his descendant George Washington Gann, who lived there. A launching ramp was built at the foot of the road. The Commercial Dock is to its south and the Harbor Marina to its north.

Penny Sedge Island (19) parallels the shore north of Gann Road. Sedge is a salt grass that grows wild on this island. Joshua Penny, another hero of the War of 1812, lived near there; thus, the name Penny Sedge Island. The town owns the northern 4.6 acres, and the Harbor Marina owns the southern 1.1 acres of the island.

Flaggy Hole Road (20) is named after blue flag, an iris that grows in wetlands. Abigail E. Field, who lived there in the early 1900s, recalled seeing blue flags near the watering hole for cattle at the end of this road.

Blue Bay Girl Scout Camp (21), north of Flaggy Hole Road, is situated on land once owned by Isaac Edwards in the 1800s. His tombstone is still on the corner of Three Mile Harbor and Flaggy

Hole Road. This was also the site of the Franklin Farm until the 1940s. In 1947, the Nassau County Girl Scouts purchased the land for $19,000 from James Gerard. By 1962, the camp had acquired a total of 179 acres, a combination of woods and beachfront on Gardiner's Bay. The camp can accommodate a total of 800 campers during its summer season. The ages of the girls range from 5 to 16, and most come from Nassau County. Not all the girls are Girl Scouts, but those who are may earn badges while there. The activities include group interaction, sports, crafts, boating, swimming, and nature study.

Maidstone Park (22) is Town-owned parkland on the east side of the entry to Three Mile Harbor. In the 1850s, when it was owned by Daniel Sherrill Edwards, it was part of a working farm used primarily for an ox pasture. Frederick and Amy Gallatin, homeowners near Hook Pond in the Village, bought this property in 1895 by Gardiner's Bay primarily to house their horses and to provide a landing for their yacht. Their seagoing yacht *Amy*, with its crew of 33 men, moored a mile offshore because Three Mile Harbor was too shallow. In 1898, Frederick let the government use his boat in the Spanish-American War. The Gallatins eventually deeded their 22.6 acres to East Hampton for one

dollar in 1911, on the condition that it be used as parkland and that there be no concessions there. Gallatin Lane was named in their honor. The park's calm waters of the bay beach, its barbeque facilities at the pavilion (the former stable), and the ball field make it a popular summer spot. In 1923, a total of 4,672 people used the park. Sunday School picnics were held there. Mary Louise Dodge noted that her weekly bath was a swim at Maidstone Park on Saturdays during the summer to be clean for Sunday. The old pavilion by the ball field was torn down in 1950, and a new pavilion with grills and picnic tables and restrooms was built near the jetty. It is still a favorite gathering place for young and old.

Hog Creek (23), an inlet on Gardiner's Bay northeast of Three Mile Harbor, was mentioned in records as early as 1655. Its steep shores and shallow water made it a favorite place for settlers to let their pigs "waller" in the mud. Hog Creek Highway was established in the mid-1800s to connect Springs Fireplace Road to Hog Creek.

Lion Head (24), a rock so named for its shape, is located in Gardiner's Bay just north of Hog Creek's inlet. Lion Head is also a residential area west of Hog Creek. Its entry road is named Isle of Wight, the original name of Gardiner's Island. Historically, **Low Hollow (25)** (between Hog Creek Point and Kings Point Road) was the site for communicating with Gardiner's Island. A bonfire would be lighted on the shore, and the smoke would signal to someone on Gardiner's Island that a boat was needed for a pick-up. A reenactment of this bonfire was held in 1948 as part of the 300th Anniversary of the founding of East Hampton Township. Fireplace Road is named for this practice.

Kings Point (26), to the east of Hog Creek Point on Gardiner's Bay, was said to have been the place where an early settler by the name of King made his home in 1649. It was said that when King's fire died out, he walked to East Hampton to bring back burning coal to start another fire. To keep the coal lit, he fed it with dry brush as he walked back.

Abraham's Path (27), located south of the Head of the Harbor, is the old road connecting Three Mile Harbor and Amagansett, a distance of three miles. It is named for Abraham Schellinger, an early settler in Amagansett in 1690. His father was Jacobus, a Dutch merchant who came to live in East Hampton after the Dutch were defeated in 1664 by the English. His stepson, James Loper,

Left: Swimming lessons for "guppies" at Maidstone Park in July (Photo by Diane C. Hewett)
Background Sketch: "View from Sunset Cove" by Carl Scorza, 1989
Right: An osprey building its nest on a nesting platform at Maidstone Park (Photo by Diane C. Hewett)

joined the family in their whaling enterprises. Abraham and his brother, Jacob, wanted to have their own farms, so they settled in Amagansett along with their sister, Catherine, and her husband, Nathaniel Baker. Abraham Schellinger was captain of the sloop the *Endeavor*. He sailed between Northwest Harbor in East Hampton and Boston in the 1700s, trading cattle, sheep, horses, and whale oil for merchandise from the West Indies. Abraham Schellinger became the first Supervisor of East Hampton in 1700. Abraham's Landing is also named for him.

Round Swamp (28) is on Three Mile Harbor Road, heading south to town. It has been farmed by the Lester family for generations and is now the site of the family's popular Round Swamp Farm. Carolyn Lester Snyder runs the farmstand with help from a lot of other Lesters, including her sister Diane and her cousin by marriage Gayle. Carolyn's parents were Barbara and Albert Lester. Albert was the son of Fred and Winifred Lester. Next to the farmstand is the original Lester house, built in the

1770s of white oak in a mortise and tenon construction. Carolyn Snyder has renovated the old house and lives there with her family. On the tombstones in a cemetery south of the farmstand can be found many old East Hampton names, such as Lester, Bennett, Miller, and others.

Freetown (29), at the southern end of Three Mile Harbor Road, was an area partially inhabited by enslaved Africans who were freed by the Gardiner family around 1806. When other slaves were freed in the 1830s, they were given land there as well.

The area was also used to relocate Montauk Indians. Developer Arthur W. Benson of the Brooklyn Gas Company purchased 11,000 acres of land in Montauk from the original proprietors' descendants in 1879. He resettled Indians from Indian Field in Montauk to land between Three Mile Harbor Road and Fireplace Road, which he had bought at a tax sale, deeding each Indian family a small plot of land (about 1/4 acre). After their move, the old homesteads in Montauk were all destroyed except for one, which was moved to North Main Street/Three Mile Harbor Road for Maria Pharaoh's family. The Pharaohs, Fowlers, Butlers, Wrights, and Hortons are some of the Indian families who were resettled.

Poverty, lack of education, and disease in Freetown gave rise to what is now known as the **Neighborhood House (30).** Trying to alleviate some of the problems in Freetown, Mr. George Eldridge began a Sunday School at St. Matthew Chapel in 1890, located opposite the current Neighborhood House. He was helped by Mrs. Theodore Weston, a summer resident, who in turn enlisted Mrs. Mary Gustine in 1892 to head the project.

Their work attracted the attention of Mr. and Mrs. Frederick Gallatin and Dr. and Mrs. Everett Herrick. In 1909, the Gallatins bought land on Three Mile Harbor Road, built a house, and deeded it to the First Presbyterian Church as the Settlement House for social work. Their funding helped establish a preschool there in 1915.

In 1917, diphtheria threatened to be an epidemic. Springs children with diphtheria were quarantined at home for five months. Hospitals would not admit them. Local medical aid was desperately needed. Dr. David Edwards treated them in his house south of Hook Mill by removing their tonsils to eliminate diphtheria germs. Mrs. J. M. Hodson built a small clinic next to the Settlement House, and Mrs. S. K. Martin helped equip it. Mary Louise Dodge remembers having her tonsils removed there as a child.

In 1920, the Settlement House and Emergency Hospital were incorporated under the name East Hampton Visiting Nurse Association. A much-needed addition to the clinic was built in 1925, thanks to Mrs. Hodson, Miss Mary Thompson, and Mr. Lorenzo Woodhouse. Without the help of these caring people, the situation in Freetown would have been desperate. In 1929, the title and deed to the property were transferred to the East Hampton Visiting Nurse Association.

Although the hospital was discontinued in the 1940s, the community services continued. In 1982, the association's name was changed to East Hampton Neighborhood House Association. Community programs, youth services, and meeting rooms are still provided, benefiting all the townspeople of East Hampton.

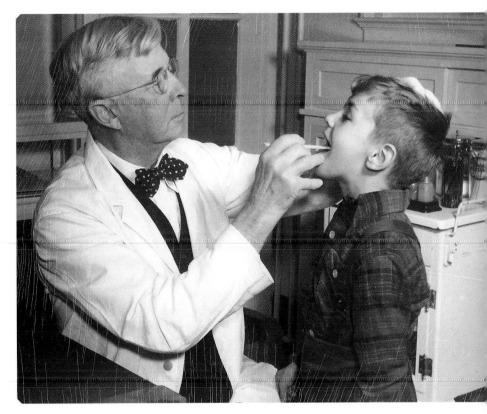

The intersection of Three Mile Harbor Road, Fireplace Road, and North Main Street is an area known as **Sandy Hook (31).** This triangular piece of land is now owned by East Hampton Town and is kept as parkland. Flowers are tended there by the Eastern Gate Garden Club. A flowering cherry tree in spring and a huge lighted Christmas tree in December welcome people to the Springs and Three Mile Harbor.

***Above:** Dr. David Edwards treating the tonsils of Lyndon English (Photo by Dave Edwardes, courtesy of Ann Roberts)*
***Below:** A flowering cherry tree at Sandy Hook, the land between the fork formed by Three Mile Harbor Road and Fireplace Road (Photo by Diane C. Hewett)*
***Facing Page:** Round Swamp Farm is a favorite spot for local fish and produce. (Photo by Diane C. Hewett)*

Indian Settlements

*P*aumanock, the Indian name for Long Island, meaning "Land of Tribute," was settled with members of the Algonquin (Algonkian) tribe east of what is now known as Brooklyn, where the Canarsie tribe was located. These Algonquins settled in thirteen locations on Long Island, with the Montaukets on the easternmost end of the island.

Montauk is not a tribal name but a description of the place where the Indians lived. Montauk is from *meus-ta-cut*, meaning "at the fort," or "fortified place."

The Montauket Indians were under tribute to the Pequot Indians of New England and also to the English. They paid the English taxes for protection from other warring tribes and for the right to trade.

In winter, the Montaukets chose campsites near Three Mile Harbor, where they fished and hunted, made wampum, and enjoyed the sheltered shores with fresh water bubbling up out of the ground. The Indians would hollow out a log and place it over a spring, creating a cistern for fresh water for their horses and cows as well as for personal use. Springy Banks Road takes its name from this natural phenomenon. There was an old dirt trail that paralleled the western shoreline, called "Indian Highway," where Hampton Waters Development is now.

One favorite Indian site was located between the forked waters of Hands Creek on the western shore of the Harbor. Indians called it Ashawagh, meaning "a place between." The camp was about an acre in size. Town Records mention the name Ashawagh as early as 1666. Springs used this name for their community hall. In 1847, Springs used Ashawagh Hall as a schoolhouse. A larger school building was constructed on School Street in 1909, but it burned down in 1929. During its reconstruction, classes were held in Ashawagh Hall once again.

Three Mile Harbor's sheltered shores had abundant clams, mussels, periwinkles, whelks, scallops, oysters, and eels. The Indians benefited from the abundance of fish and shellfish not only for food, but also from the shells which were made into wampum (seawant or peague). The manufacture of wampum as a medium of exchange was one of Long Island's major industries.

Many archaeological digs were made by the New York State, Suffolk County, and Long Island Archaeological Associations from the 1920s to the 1970s, supervised by C. Johanneman, Roy Latham, A. Schroeder, Arthur Parker, John Strong, and Foster Saville. There were many Niantic and Sebonac campsites by the southeastern shore of the Harbor near Springy Banks and Hampton Waters, Soak Hides, Copeces, Shagwong, and Squaw Cove. They found many hearths and pits, along with shell midden (broken pieces), trade sherd (pottery pieces), fishhooks, mortars, pestles, arrowheads, and stone artifacts in these areas. There were eleven separate sites recorded along the shores of the Harbor. An arrowhead was found in 1998 along the western shores by a hiker.

Squaw Cove, on the northeastern side of Three Mile Harbor, was sited by archaeologists with extensive shell heaps called midden. Squaw Cove's shell heap was 180 feet by 25 feet and 26 inches deep, as documented by an investigation in 1927 by The Museum of the American Indian.

Making wampum money was traditionally the job of the women; hence, the name "Squaw Cove." Wampum was made from hard clams and whelks. The inside hinge of the hard clam *(quahaug)* shell provided the black wampum *(sucki)*. Purple and white wampum was made from the rest of the clam shell and from whelk shells. The black wampum was considered twice as valuable as the white. The inner core of the whelk was also used, since it was already cylindrical and smooth.

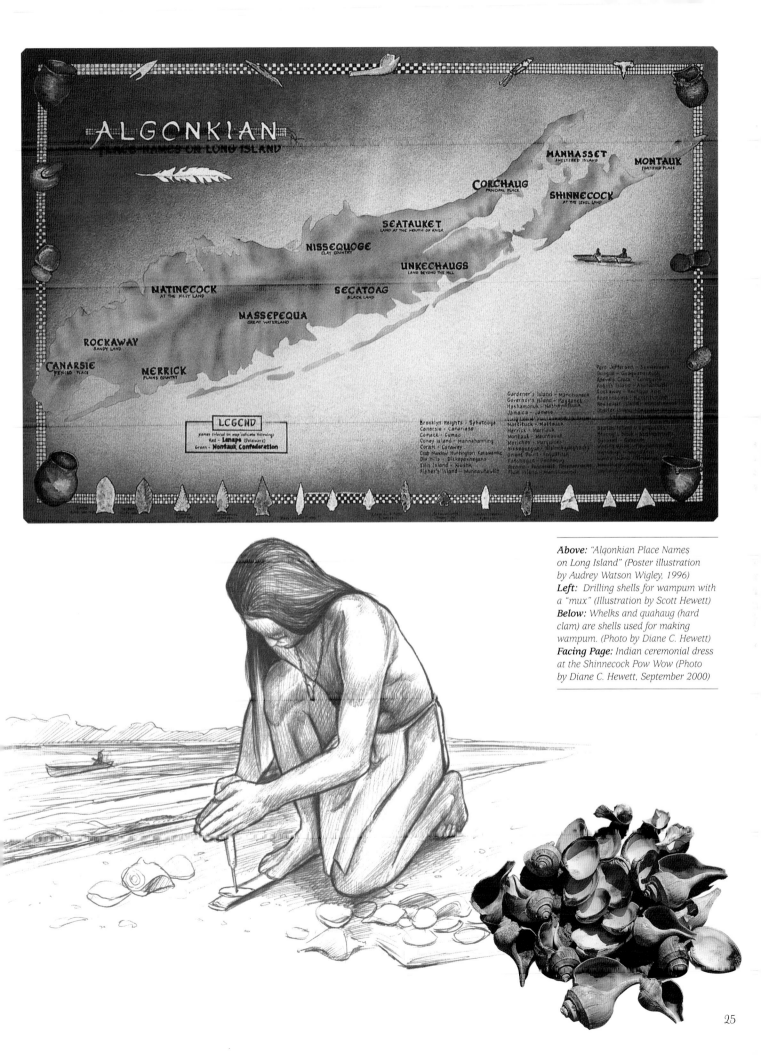

Above: "Algonkian Place Names on Long Island" (Poster illustration by Audrey Watson Wigley, 1996)
Left: Drilling shells for wampum with a "mux" (Illustration by Scott Hewett)
Below: Whelks and quahaug (hard clam) are shells used for making wampum. (Photo by Diane C. Hewett)
Facing Page: Indian ceremonial dress at the Shinnecock Pow Wow (Photo by Diane C. Hewett, September 2000)

Right: Princess Pocahontas Pharaoh, daughter of Chief David Pharaoh, a descendant of Wyandanch, was born in 1879 and lived in Freetown. This picture, taken in 1940, shows her holding a "scrub" that she carved from wood. (From the Red Thundercloud Collection at East Hampton Library)

Facing Page

Above: *An example of an Indian barne—an 1850 picture of John Henry Thompson standing in front of an Indian cellar used for food storage (Red Thundercloud Collection at East Hampton Library)*

Below: *Brochure from the Southold Indian Museum (Incorporated Long Island Chapter, New York State Archaeological Association; Illustration and design by the late Arthur F. Sammartino)*

An important tool needed to make the wampum was a mux, a metal drill used to make holes in the shells. Muxes were such valuable tools for the Indians that they were included in the items offered to the Indians when East Hampton was sold to the early settlers.

A popular source of food for the Indians was ground nuts, a potatolike root *(Apios tuberosa)*, which grew in abundance in Acabonack. *Acabonack* means "place where the nuts are." *Sagaponack* means "place where the big nuts are."

The Montaukets were also farmers, growing corn, squash, beans, cucumbers, and tobacco. They fertilized their crops with menhaden, an oily fish. Farming was the work of the old and the very young. Hunting and fishing occupied the men, and the women tended the camp, made wampum, and cared for the children. Food was dried and stored in Indian "barnes," four to five foot deep holes in the ground that were covered with sticks. These holes preserved the food from freezing during the winter and kept food cool in the summer.

In order to have a readily available supply of meat, snare traps were constructed. Trees were placed in a V formation a half mile long, which funneled deer into a snare at the point. The deer were trapped and kept alive until the tribe needed the meat.

Birds and fowl were very abundant. An observer wrote, "wild pigeons continued flying for four or five hours together; one could not see the beginning or ending—length or breadth of these millions of millions."

Every spring, the Indians burned the underbrush and trees, allowing for ease of planting and hunting. Ticks were also eliminated this way. There was a shortage of large timber for this reason, but extensive meadowland. This practice of burning stopped when early settlers arrived and needed wood for building and fuel.

Indian summer houses were tentlike; but in winter, they constructed one great house in which many could live together, with a fireplace in the center for heating and cooking.

Two types of boats were used. One was made from a huge log as long as 60 feet, the inside of which was burned and scraped out with clam shells. The other boat, light and sleek, was built from the bark of birch trees and was easily carried overland.

The Indian Museum in Southold, New York, has a collection on view of arrowheads from Three Mile Harbor, along with wampum, pots, pipes, and other artifacts. 🔥

Organized in 1925—Incorporated in 1948

Discover the
Indian
Museum
Southold, N.Y.

New York State
Archaeological Association
Long Island Chapter Incorporated
Bayview Road, Southold, N.Y.
P.O. Box 268, Southold, NY 11971

East Hampton's Settlers

*M*any pious people were trying to escape religious persecution in Europe and were intent on finding true religious freedom in America. They also came here seeking land for their cattle and, above all, to be independent landowners. Landownership was equated with status and wealth. Whenever freemen could acquire property to develop for themselves, they rarely wished to work for anyone else.

In 1630, eleven ships with 1,700 people left Southampton, England, for the "New England." Some went to Boston; some to Salem; some to Lynn, Massachusetts; and others to Hartford, New Haven, and Wethersfield, Connecticut. By 1643, more than 200 ships had sailed from England for the Massachusetts Bay Colony with some 21,000 more people.

Unfortunately, their troubles were not left behind in England. Their first winter was so severe, with storms lasting from November to April, that most of their livestock died. The following summer's intolerable heat prevented successful crops. A severe earthquake on June 1, 1638, Indian attacks, and an outbreak of influenza further added to their hardships. In 1646, a black caterpillar infestation destroyed the corn, wheat, and barley. In November of that year, there was a hurricane. To say that life was hard is an understatement. It was devastating!

They had hoped for freedom of worship in this new land, but the Puritans of Plymouth Colony were "rigid separatists." They wanted to separate themselves from the Church of England and its practices. These congregational churches levied taxes for their support and would not allow "outsiders" to vote or take a freeman's oath (an oath swearing to be an inhabitant and subject to the local government). Traditions of the Church of England were forbidden, such as celebrating Christmas, saying prayers, baptizing infants, reading the Bible, displaying crosses, celebrating the resurrection at Easter, and so on.

In 1636, Roger Williams was banished for his religious beliefs. He left Boston to establish Rhode Island. Anne Hutchinson was also excommunicated and banished in 1638. She and her family also sought refuge in Rhode Island at Aquidneck Island. After her husband died, she moved to what is now Pelham, New York, where she and all but one of her children were massacred in an Indian attack.

This map of England depicts the origins of East Hampton's settlers. (Source: East Hampton Star *article "Speaking Bonac —Echoes of Dorset," by Isabelle Norton, April 28, 1977)*

The Massachusetts Bay Colony had received a charter from England in 1629, allowing for the establishment of settlements, or "plantations," on Long Island, or "Paumanock." John Winthrop had called the colonization of Massachusetts Bay a project of human labor in which spiritual and material ends were co-joined.

Many merchants and traders even had investments in several colonies. Among them was John Winthrop, Governor of the Massachusetts Bay Colony. After starting the initial settlement, the investors actively recruited other settlers to make their plantation thrive, because a thriving settlement meant a good return on their money.

The years between 1630 and 1643 were known as "The Great Migration." Although discouraged by the Royal Proclamation of Charles I in 1637 to restrict migration, many people left England anyway.

The search for a place to be free from intolerance and the desire to establish themselves as land owners resulted in the desertion of more than 300 acres in Lynn, Massachusetts, by 1640. Popular destinations were eastern Pennsylvania and Long Island. The Dutch prevented them from settling in the western end of Long Island, so they claimed territory on the eastern end. Aiding these settlements was Captain Daniel Howe, a former lieutenant in the Pequot Wars. He led groups of people eager to resettle on Long Island. In 1640, he sailed his ship from Lynn to settle Southampton. Eight years later, he helped establish East Hampton. The "planters" that came with him to East Hampton were John Stratton, Thomas Talmage, Jr., Thomas Tomson, John Hand, John and William Mulford, Robert Bond, and possibly Joshua Barnes and Robert Rose.

The Town Records of 1655 list additional settlers, including Fulk Davis, Thomas Osborne, Jr., Thomas Osborne, Sr., William Hedges, Jeremy Meecham, Robert Rose (his widow later married Ananias Conkling), Thomas James (the minister), Lion Gardiner, Thomas Chatfield, Ralph Dayton, Benjamin Price, William Edwards, William Simons, Samuel Parsons, Samuel Belknap, William Barnes, Nathaniel Bishop, Vincent Meigs, Joshua Garlick, Richard Brooks, William Fithian, Richard Stratton, Luke Lillie, and Thomas Baker (who bought Daniel Howe's house). Although women settled here also, women's names were not included in the public record. Descendants of some of these settlers live in East Hampton today.

Captain Howe, who was also a surveyor, probably surveyed and laid out plots for their village. These men and their families called the village Maidstone after a port in Kent, England, on the Medway River, about ten miles upriver from the North Sea. The settlers changed the name of the town to East Hampton shortly thereafter. (*Hampton* means "field.") The site of the original village is where present-day East Hampton Village's flagpole, cemetery, and Town Pond are located.

Captain Edward Johnson wrote in his 1653 historical writings of Southampton and East Hampton, "The poorest person hath a house and land of his own and bread of his own growing."

Captain Daniel Howe, a landowner of 60 acres in Lynn, didn't stay long in East Hampton. In 1648, he built a house in East Hampton, but he lived on Gardiner's Island tending cattle until 1653. Having no use for his house in East Hampton, he sold it in 1650 to Thomas Baker, who used the house for a meetinghouse and "Ordinary."

Robert Bond, who was well educated, helped organize the local government, drawing up deeds, pacts, and other legal documents between the settlers and the Indians and also handled the settlers' dealings with the Connecticut government.

John Hand, Sr., formerly a landowner in Kent, England, came first to Southampton and then moved to East Hampton with his wife, Alice Gransden, and their six children. He signed "yeoman" as his trade. Active in East Hampton government, in 1657 he was sent as a delegate to Hartford to have the Connecticut system of government adopted for East Hampton. In Hartford, he also attended the trial of Goody Garelick, who was accused of witchcraft. His son, Stephen Hand, is recorded on a 1660 Indian deed and again in the Dongan Patent of 1686 (see page 33). Hand's Creek and Stephen Hand's Path are named for these early settlers.

Illustration by Scott Hewett

Thomas Talmage, Jr., was a descendant of an old English family, Toelmag, from the sixth century. His father, Thomas Talmage, Sr., from the County of Southampton or Hampshire, England, came to Lynn, Massachusetts in 1630 with his five children, where he owned 200 acres. Thomas Talmage, Jr., moved to East Hampton and became the first Recorder, or Town Clerk, for the Town of East Hampton.

John Mulford came from South Molton, Devonshire, near Barnstable, a busy port that supplied wares between Newfoundland and Boston. He settled first in Salem, then Southampton, and finally in East Hampton. John was the son of Judge John Mulford, and they shared the same house here. John Mulford distinguished himself as one of the signers of the Dongan Patent of 1686 (see page 33).

Samuel Mulford, the eldest son of Judge John Mulford, was a merchant dealing in whale oil, who fought its excessive tax in England. His nickname, "Fish-hooks," came from his practice of sewing fishhooks in his pockets to thwart pickpockets in London. In East Hampton, he purchased a house that Josiah Hobart had built near the Town Pond. This dwelling is now the Mulford Museum on James Lane.

Thomas Osborne, Sr., who had been a resident of New Haven, moved with his sons, Thomas and Benjamin, to East Hampton sometime around 1650. The name Thomas Osborne is listed on a 1641 map, "The Nine Squares of New Haven." 🖋

A 1676 English map of Long Island by J. Speed, borrowed from Richard B. Arkway, Inc., in New York City (Courtesy of the East Hampton Historical Society)

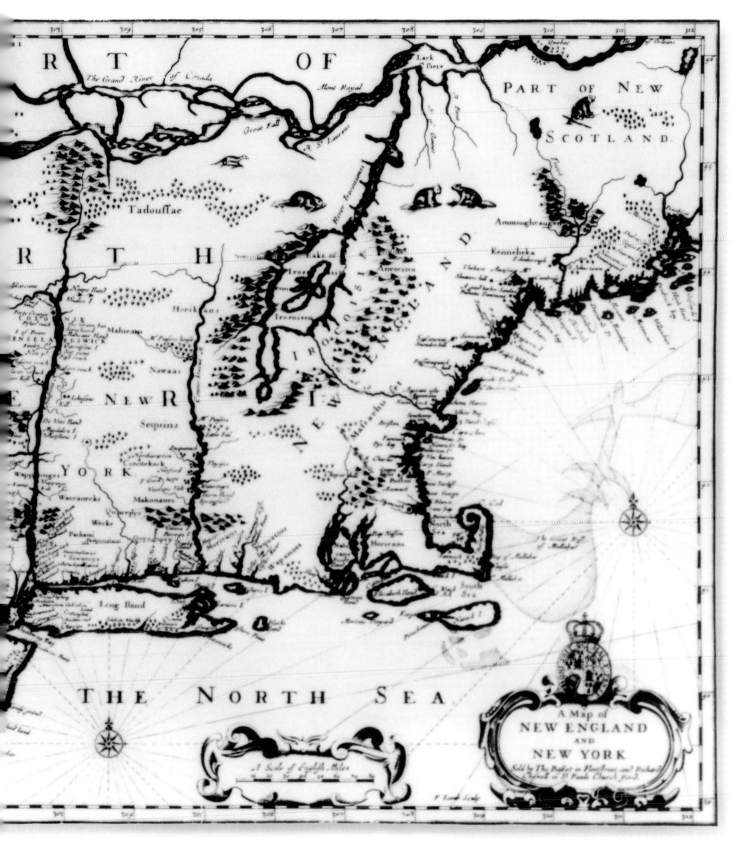

East Hampton Town Founded

*K*ing James I of England had issued a patent to the Plymouth Company in 1620 for the territory called New England. The Plymouth Council granted patents to Plymouth in 1621, to Massachusetts and Connecticut in 1631, and to Long Island in April 1635. The Long Island Patent was granted to William Alexander, the Earl of Sterling, who assigned James Farrett as his agent. Farrett, due to lack of funds, had to mortgage his holdings on Long Island to Governors Eaton and Hopkins. These two English governors, Theophilus Eaton of New Haven and Edward Hopkins of Connecticut, with the help of Lion Gardiner, purchased all the land from the Southampton borders to Hither Hills in Montauk from the Grand Sachem, Wyandanch. Wyandanch — representing the Montauk, Shinnecock, Corchake, and Monhansuck-Ahaquazuwamuck (Algonquin) Indians — was anxious to have the protection of the English from the enemies of the Algonquins and to have good trade relations with the English. He therefore sold these 31,000 acres on April 29, 1648, for 20 coats; 24 each of hatchets, hoes, knives, and looking glasses; and 100 "muxes," or awls.

Wyandanch's sign, used on a 1655 deed with the "Towne of EastHampton," as recorded in Thomas Cooper's book The Records of the Court of Sessions of Suffolk County in the Province of New York 1670–1688

Wyandanch represented the Indians because of an agreement in 1645 between the four Sachems of Paumanock, who were all brothers. They also protected any weak tribes who requested their help. Chief Wyandanch of Montauk became the Chief Sachem of Paumanock after his brother's death in 1652. His manual sign was considered necessary for transferring land deeds from the Indians to the early settlers. The name Wyandanch means "wise speaker." His leadership resulted in peaceful relations with the settlers.

The Puritans' settlements were organized into landholding systems in which initial investors contributed capital and political security to their endeavor. Allotments of land were made to the settlers depending on the amount of investment the settler had made in the "plantation." Unallocated land was owned by the paying founders according to their initial investment.

The East Hampton government was pure democracy, adapted to the sparse population and the simple lives led here. The decision-making power was in the assemblies at the Town Meetings, called the General Court. A blast of gunshot and a roll of the drums signaled the assembly of meetings. Every man was required to attend or be fined. During these meetings, laws were made, disputes settled, and moral matters judged.

Because the settlers governed themselves, they regarded themselves as independent. Even though they were not under the auspices of Connecticut, they still felt connected to its people and democratic philosophy.

In 1650, Robert Bond, on behalf of the settlers, went to Connecticut to get "evidence for our land an acquittance for payment of money and for a body of laws." He was chosen, along with John Hand, Thomas Baker, and John Mulford, to carry on the affairs of the Town.

In 1651, Connecticut Governors Eaton and Hopkins officially assigned the land bought from Chief Wyandanch in 1648 to the residents of East Hampton for 30 pounds, 4 shillings, and 6 pence.

This deed for "the inhabitants of East Hampton" was signed by nine men: John Hand, Sr., John Stratton, Sr., Thomas Talmage, Jr., Robert Bond, Daniel Howe, Robert Rose, Thomas Tomson, Joshua Barnes, and John Mulford.

In 1664, the English won their battle with the Dutch, and New Netherlands became New York. New York became a proprietary colony of James II, the Duke of York and brother of King Charles II. East Hampton was annexed to the New York Colony, separating it from Connecticut's rule. Richard Nicolls, Lieutenant Governor General under the Duke of York, issued a patent on March 13, 1666, granting the inhabitants of East Hampton "all the privileges belonging to a town within this border."

Unfortunately, Nicolls had trouble governing the independently minded people of East Hampton. The townspeople objected to the laws imposed upon them. Nicolls tried to establish a centralized government in New York for the towns on Long Island, but he left in 1668 without accomplishing

his goal. He was replaced by Francis Lovelace, who tried to establish control over the whale oil trade and, with the Assize of 1670, tried to control other trading. Hogs could be butchered only in New York City, assuring the collection of taxes. East Hampton would not comply and butchered their hogs for sale here in town. Lovelace was then replaced by Sir Edmund Andros, who was to deal with the "rebel" towns. In 1683, Thomas Dongan was sent by the Duke of York to govern the colonies.

Taxation without representation was addressed to the Duke of York in a speech in 1685, given by Thomas James, John Mulford, and Thomas and William Talmage. An assembly was ultimately established, which involved the towns on Long Island. A New York Charter of "Libertyes and Priviledges" established rights to a trial by jury, permission to hold property without illegal interference, and freedom of religion for Christians.

Thomas Dongan, the Governor General of the New York Colony, issued the Dongan Patent on December 9, 1686, thereby assuring East Hampton its proprietary ownership, the additional purchase of 10,000 acres in Montauk, the creation of a Board of Trustees, and the rights of freeholders to elect their own representatives. With this patent, the people of East Hampton were achieving a stronger voice in their government. The establishment of the Trustees in East Hampton granted them control over public lands and inland waters. This important document was signed on behalf of the freeholders and inhabitants of East Hampton by Thomas

James, Josiah Hobart, Thomas Talmage, John Wheeler, Samuel and John Mulford, Thomas Chatfield, Sr., Jeremiah Conklin, Stephen Hand, Robert Dayton, Thomas Baker, and Thomas Osborne. These twelve men were the forerunners of our current Trustees, a group elected by the townspeople of East Hampton.

Governor Dongan reported in 1687 that "Most of the people of the island, especially towards the East, are of the same stamp as those of New England, refractory and very loath to have any commerce with this place New York to the great detriment of his Majesty's revenue and ruin of our merchants."

When King Charles II died in 1685, his brother James II established the Dominion of New England. He revoked the New York Charter and established the old system of a governor and a council instead. Representation in the government ended, and East Hampton became subservient to the New York government once more.

This dissension over the right to govern oneself festered in America until it culminated in the "War of Independence" from England in 1776. ♦

The Gardiner Heritage

The influence of Lion Gardiner in the establishment of the Town of East Hampton cannot be underestimated. Lion Gardiner was a surveyor and military engineer in Holland. In 1635, he was sent by Lord Say and Sele and Lord Brook on behalf of the Crown of England to lay out a fort at the mouth of the Connecticut River. The project, called Saybrook, was under the governorship of John Winthrop. Gardiner made the trip across the Atlantic in his ship Batcheler, accompanied by his wife, Mary (Marrichen Duercant from Woerden); her maid, Eliza Colet; and twelve men. It was an extremely difficult voyage, and disaster was awaiting them in Connecticut.

Troubles plagued Gardiner at Saybrook due to lack of supplies, a fierce winter, trouble with the Pequot Indians, and his disagreements with the English authorities. He finally gave up the "Saybrook Project" and tried to find a place of his own. Gardiner had a friend and ally in Wyandanch, chief of the Montauk Indians, who suggested an island close to East Hampton, called Manchonake, meaning "the place where many have died." Hundreds of Indians had died there either from war with a Connecticut tribe or from fever.

Lion took a liking to this island close to East Hampton and moved there in 1639 with his wife and two children, David and Mary. He called the island Isle of Wight, after an island of the same shape off the coast of England across the English Channel from Cherbourg. Gardiner bought the island from the Sachem of Manhansuk, Youcoe (Youghe), and his wife, Aswaw. Youcoe was the elder brother of Wyandanch and was later called Poggatacut. Gardiner purchased the island from the Indians for ten coats of trading cloth, but he was also careful to get a grant from James Farrett, the agent of the Earl of Sterling, to validate his purchase. Farrett conveyed the island "which he hath now in his possession, which island hath been purchased before my coming, from the ancient inhabitants, the Indians."

Gardiner was active in the government of East Hampton from its beginnings. He moved his family to the town in 1653, needing the security of the town due to the warring Narragansett Indians from Connecticut who were both a danger to the early settlers and to the Montauk Indians.

The good relationship between the Montauks, Wyandanch, and Lion resulted in guarded, but peaceful, relations between the Montauks and the East Hampton townspeople. Lion protected Wyandanch from false accusations by the English regarding the murder of a Southampton woman, Phebe Halsey, and assisted the Montauks in their wars against the Narragansetts with promises of protection.

Chief Wyandanch's enemy, Ninigret, sachem of the Niantic tribe, raided his village in Montauk, killing about thirty men and seizing his daughter, Quashawam, along with fourteen other captives. Gardiner helped raise the money for Quashawam's ransom, resulting in her release. On other occasions, he enlisted the help of the English for the protection of Wyandanch's tribe.

Relations were stable until a series of events occurred: the death of Wyandanch in 1659, the death of Lion Gardiner in 1663, the English conquest of New Netherlands in 1664 establishing New York, and the great plague that killed two thirds of the Algonquin people on Long Island between 1659 and 1664.

After Lion Gardiner died, his son, David (second proprietor), inherited the island. When David died in 1689, his son, John (third proprietor), became Lord of the Island.

In 1686, Governor Dongan tried to annex Gardiner's Island to the Town of East Hampton, but he did not succeed. He did grant tax relief and independent jurisdiction of the Isle of Wight, decreeing "one lordship and manor of Gardiner's Island." Gardiner's Island was annexed to East Hampton and New York State in 1788 by the General Assembly of New York. Today, the island is held in trust for the direct descendants, Robert David Lion Gardiner and his niece, Alexandra Gardiner Creel Goelet. They have inherited a real treasure and also a responsibility to maintain and preserve its singularity.

The Gardiner-Brown House, on Main Street in the Village, was built in 1740 by David Gardiner (sixth

Above: The Gardiner Crest; this documentation is on the back of the mounting: "The Arms of the family of Gardiner of Gardiner's Island, State of N.Y. [stated in "Bank of Baronage" to be the heirs to the ancient Baronies of Fitz Allan and Fitz Malter.] Argent (white) a Chevron between three horns Gules (red) garnished Or (gold) string – Sable (black) = Crest a Dexter arm armed, the hand Proper grasping a broken staff Gules. A George fecit, 203 Broadway, N.Y." (Courtesy of Isabel Gardiner Mairs)

Facing Page
Clockwise From Top Left:
Grave of Lion Gardiner in East Hampton Town Cemetery (Photo by Diane C. Hewett) • Gardiner's Island map, by artist Jean Held, South Fork Natural History Society, SOFO booklet Vol. 6 #1, 1994; Gardiner's Island is the oldest estate owned by a single family in the United States. • An osprey's nest, possibly built on Gardiner's Island (Photo courtesy of Isabel Gardiner Mairs) • Thomas Gardiner's 1835 White House. (Photo courtesy of Isabel Gardiner Mairs) • Postcards from Winthrop Gardiner, dated 1907 (Courtesy of Isabel Gardiner Mairs)

THE
RUINS
*site of old
Fort Tyler*

*This
peninsula
disappeared
in the late
1800s*

BOSTWICK
POINT

BOSTWICK
BAY

Canoe
Place or
Stepping-
stone
Stream

CROW
HEAD

Bostwick
Creek

EASTERN
POINT

BOSTWICK FOREST

Cherry
Hill
Pond

CAPTAIN
KIDD
MONUMENT

MANOR
HOUSE

Wolfies
Hole

WHALE
HILL

Willow
Brook

Lily
Pond

Home
Pond

WIND-
MILL

Gaylor
Hole

ROGERS
WOODS

Garlick
Pond

CHERRY HILL
POINT

CHERRY
HARBOR

TOBACCOLOT
BAY

Tobaccolot
Pond

Little
Pond

GARDINERS
BAY

Gales
Pond

Airport
Pond

Great
Pond

NAPEAGUE
BAY

CARTW
RIGHT
ISLAND
one mile south

proprietor). He lived there with his wife, Rachel née Schellinger. In 1924, Winthrop Gardiner had it moved back from Main Street for more privacy. The house is currently owned by the Ladies' Village Improvement Society.

Another house was built on Main Street in East Hampton by Thomas Gardiner in 1835. This house, named the White House, was destroyed following the 1938 hurricane and was rebuilt in an Italian style by Sarah Diodati Gardiner. Robert D.L. Gardiner currently lives there. His cousin Isabel Gardiner Mairs lives close by on James Lane, near the historic sarcophagus of Lion Gardiner in the old south end cemetery of East Hampton. This family has long been intertwined with the history of East Hampton. 🍂

Three Mile Harbor's Settlers

*T*he first settler along the shores of Three Mile Harbor was **John Gann.** He arrived with Lord Lion Gardiner — first in Connecticut, then to Gardiner's Island in 1639, and finally settled along Three Mile Harbor in 1640. John Gann and his brother-in-law **Samuel Bennett** lived by Soak Hides and Will Curl Highway. Other Ganns lived by Squaw Cove on the northeastern shore of Three Mile Harbor.

a witch. She was subjected to a dunking in Town Pond as a test to see if she was indeed in league with the Devil. It is said that when she was widowed and old, Gardiner felt sorry for Goody and gave her a cottage on his island in which to live out her days.

Town Records indicate that other early landowners on the eastern side of Three Mile Harbor were **Vincent Meigs, John Mulford, Robert Bond, John Myller, Thomas Osborne, Sr., William Miller, Thomas Chatfield, Thomas Baker, Jeremiah Miller, Thomas Edwards, and Jeremiah Conkling**.

On the western side of the Harbor, there was little settlement, primarily due to the lack of roads. Records show that in 1731, **Samuel and Robert Parsons** became the first owners of Sammy's Beach peninsula. The land was then sold to **Jonathan Mulford** and, in 1839, was sold to **Samuel, Henry, and Jeremiah Terry.**

The area that the Bennetts settled was called Shadom, named after the area in England from which the Bennetts originated. There is an old cemetery opposite Gardiner's Marina, south of Copeces Lane, where Bennett tombstones mark the deaths of Benjamin in 1861, Betsey in 1885, Oscar in 1879, and Frances in 1869. Interestingly, the Bennett coat of arms in England was a whelk shell, an appropriate symbol for Three Mile Harbor, with its abundance of whelks.

Another early settler of Three Mile Harbor was **Joshua Garlick,** who had a house in the village and also owned 13.5 acres on the east side of the Harbor, north of Duck Creek. He and Vincent Meigs were the town's millers. He was also a carpenter and had worked for Lion Gardiner on his island. Garlick's wife, called Goody (meaning goodwife), was accused of witchcraft in the death of Gardiner's daughter, Elizabeth. Elizabeth died soon after giving birth, and on her deathbed she had accused Goody of pricking her with pins and bewitching her with "a black thing at the foot of the bed." It is said that Gardiner interceded for Goody at her trial in Connecticut in 1658 and had saved her life. The townspeople disliked her because she was outspoken and loudmouthed, and they feared she was

An early settler just west of Sammy's Beach was **William Hedges**. In the 1700s, he had a large farm there overlooking the bay. The high bluffs are still called Hedges Banks. The farm was sold to **Henry LaFarge** in the 1870s. Whaling ships liked to anchor offshore, and the easy beach access to food and supplies near the farm became known as "LaFarges Landing."

There was a huge sheep farm that extended from Soak Hides north to Hands Creek and west to Cedar Street, worked by the family of **Benjamin Miller** from the 1700s to the early 1800s. Luckily, he had eight sons to help. His son **Isaac** lived with him on the shores between Springy Banks and Hands Creek until the house burned down. They rebuilt on Cedar Street near Miller Lane, which is named for them.

John Hand, another original settler, owned the land near Hands Creek. This was the favored winter grounds for the Indians because of its freshwater springs, shelter from the strong westerly winds, and abundant food sources. An Indian deed, dated 1660, included the name of John Hand's son **Stephen.**

A bit of the Shore, Three Mile Harbor, L. I.

The family was very active in the early government of the town. Stephen signed the Dongan Patent of 1686 that established the rights of the people to public lands and inland waters. (They certainly had a "Hand" in the early government!)

Thomas James became East Hampton's first minister in 1651. Lion Gardiner was very influential in securing him for the town. Pay for the minister was 45 pounds per year and a house. This was always supplemented with gifts from the parishioners' households, such as milk, grain, wool, eggs, and so on. Thomas James was well liked and helped with legal matters in addition to his spiritual duties.

Tho Indian language was a barrier at first for the townspeople, since there was no written language. Thomas James learned the Algonquin-Montauk language and translated for the settlers. He was a skillful mediator between the two groups.

In October 1654, James helped establish a local government by drafting, in his own hand, a version of the Connecticut Charter. Thirty freeholders from

East Hampton signed the draft, agreeing to its establishment, hoping this would give them a voice in their government

In 1686, Thomas James was jailed for preaching a sermon defending his parishioners from fraudulent accusation by the Crown of England. Despite his petition to the Governor for his release, he had to spend three weeks in prison for his "sedition."

Church was held on Sundays in the "Ordinary," or meetinghouse/tavern, which was built by Captain Howe when he first came to East Hampton. He sold it to Thomas Baker in 1651, who also lived in this all-purpose building by Town Pond. Some of this original building was preserved inside the J. Harper Poor cottage located at 181 Main Street.

When Thomas James died in 1696, he instructed in his will that he be buried facing east, possibly so that he could face his congregation on Resurrection Day and lead them into eternal life with their Lord Jesus. ❧

Above: "A bit of the Shore, Three Mile Harbor, L.I." (Postcard from the Harvey Ginsberg Collection at East Hampton Library)
Facing Page: "Launchings," a watercolor by Carl Kinscherf from the 1940s, depicts the foot of Gann Road with the Commercial Dock on the left and Hedges Banks in the distance.

Pirates and Treasures

irating was a severe threat to the East Hampton population because of their proximity to the sea and their isolation from authority. Pirates raided the Village, stealing goods and food and causing bodily harm to the population.

Above: After Captain Kidd was hung, his tarred body was put on display near London's harbor to be a deterrent to pirates.

Facing Page

Top: This image of Captain William Kidd was drawn shortly before his execution in 1701 by Sir James Thornhill. (Courtesy of East Hampton Library)

Bottom: *This cloth remnant is from an Indian cloth given to Mrs. John Lyon Gardiner by Captain William Kidd in 1699 to thank her for roasting a pig for him. The colorful design of this "Kidd blanket" was woven from silk, cotton, gold and silver threads. This cloth is on display at the East Hampton Library. (Courtesy of East Hampton Library)*

Gardiner's Island was a favorite stopping place for pirates. Captain William Kidd (1645-1701) had been authorized by the Crown of England as a privateer to capture other pirates' bounty and to raid French ships. Unfortunately, Kidd's ship, the *Adventure Galley*, captured the *Quedah Merchant*, a ship belonging to the Great Mogul. The Great Mogul showed his displeasure by making trouble with the British East India Company. The authorities in London, in trying to placate him, disowned Captain Kidd, declaring him a pirate. Kidd changed ships and, in 1699, sailed his new ship, the *San Antonio*, to Oyster Bay and then to the Isle of Wight, where he knew and trusted John Gardiner (third proprietor of Gardiner's Island). Kidd inventoried his bounty of gold, silver, and precious stones and buried the treasure in Cherry Harbor for safekeeping. He got some provisions from Gardiner and gave him gifts of muslin, silk, worsted stockings, and sugar before sailing to Boston to clear his name. Seized by Lord Bellomont (Richard Coot of Coot's Bank), he was found guilty not of piracy, but for killing his rebellious deck hand William Moore with a wooden bucket. Captain Kidd was executed on May 23, 1701, in London.

The British, wanting to make an example of him, hanged him in the public square. The rope broke with the first try, so they had to try a second time. Some people thought this was a sign of his innocence. Afterward, his body was put on display at the seashore, where waves washed over it for three days and nights. It was then tarred, enclosed in a metal framework, and hung on a high post so ships sailing in and out of London could see it as a warning to pirates.

Kidd's estate reverted to the Crown by law. John Gardiner was commanded to go to Boston with Kidd's treasure. He delivered it to Lord Bellomont in person. Some of the treasure was returned to the Crown, some was kept by Bellomont, and the rest was auctioned in the name of the Crown. The proceeds paid for 80 percent of the Royal Naval Hospital in Greenwich.

Pirates continued to be a problem for East Hampton. The white windmill on Gardiner's Island was used as a signal for East Hampton townspeople. When a pirate ship was seen, lookouts would change the vanes on the windmill from the X position to the + position. The townspeople then had a chance to hide their valuables and their women from the pirates. On Gardiner's Island, valuables were hidden down in the well. Many pirates used the island as a warehouse for their treasures and paid a fee for its storage. When a pirate died, the treasure was acquired by the Gardiners. The Gardiners benefited from this by melting down the loot and having it made into gold and silver plates by silversmiths in London. Dealing with pirates was a very risky business. In 1728, Gardiner's Island was overrun by 80 pirates who ransacked the island, tied John Gardiner to a mulberry tree, and left, leaving him badly wounded.

There is no more treasure to be found on Gardiner's Island. Local lore recounts that when the caretaker at the island wanted a boulder moved, he capitalized on rumors of treasure and buried a few coins in the sand near the boulder. Opportunity seekers soon excavated and moved the boulder, thinking there was more "treasure" to be found under it, but all they got to take home was the sand in their shoes.

Above: *Sunset view overlooking Penny Sedge Island (Photo by Edna Renner)*
Left: *The gravestone of Mary Bennet, still standing in Penny's cemetery near the shores of Three Mile Harbor on Roosevelt Avenue (Photo by Sylvia Mendelman)*

Wars, Heroes, and Habitants

*M*any wars plagued our fledgling country. The English defeated the Dutch in 1664 and New Netherlands became New York. The English and Dutch were at war for another two years, from 1672 to 1674. In the eighteenth century, the French and Indian War lasted from 1755 to 1763 and the War of Independence between the English and Americans raged from 1776 to 1783. Long Island was a captured territory ruled (abused) by the British during these seven long years. There was a second war with the English and Americans in 1812. The American Civil War (1861-1865), the aftereffects of the Spanish-American War, waged in 1898, when Teddy Roosevelt brought large numbers of typhoid-ridden and injured troops to Camp Wikoff in Montauk, and worldwide wars in the twentieth century have all affected the people here.

The townspeople of East Hampton were brave and independent, and many suffered at the hands of the British soldiers during the War of Independence. Some were torn in their allegiance to either America or England with the Declaration of Independence on July 4, 1776. After the crushing defeat of George Washington by the British on Long Island on August 27, the attitude of the people changed. The British pillaged the people here and left them with little peace or property. Their livestock and food supplies were taken, and their homes were used for housing soldiers. The church was turned into a barn. People had no rights and little means to defend themselves. The East Hampton villagers hated the English for their abuses, and they demonstrated their bravery by defying English orders and ambushing them whenever possible.

The story of the housewife who refused to give her pudding to the English troops and threw it down the hill instead is a classic example of the feisty, independent attitudes of the East Hampton people. Pudding Hill Lane in the Village is the site of this brave woman's action. Another story displaying the ingenuity of the villagers relates how they deceived the English into thinking their army was twice its size by marching by the English two times. The second time they marched past, they reversed their jackets so the colors were different. The English retreated, thinking themselves outnumbered.

The British and Americans were at war again in 1812. The British fleet in Gardiner's Bay kept a guard flotilla near Three Mile Harbor Gut (entrance), waiting to do battle in Sag Harbor. Sixteen-year-old Charles R. Hand of Amagansett was at the gut one evening and saw armed boats leave the fleet and proceed to Sag Harbor. He ran home, got his horse, and was in Sag Harbor in 40 minutes, warning the militia there to repulse the attack. Not only did they succeed in doing so, they also captured one boat filled with ammunition.

Two sailors from Three Mile Harbor, John Gann and Joshua Penny, were seized on the seas and made to serve in the British Navy. Joshua Penny was impressed by the British Navy against his will for fifteen years and finally escaped. He hated the British for this inscription and tried to thwart the enemy any way he could. On July 26, 1813, he was commissioned by General Decatur in New London to pilot a force of four boats to Gardiner's Island, where the British had troops. He took eight men as prisoners and was paid forty dollars. A month later, he was asked to pilot a torpedo boat to Sag Harbor to destroy the British ships, among them the *Ramilies,* with 74 cannons, and the *Orpheus.* Eight miles from Sag Harbor, a fierce storm drove their ship ashore and the keel was broken. The crew hid the torpedo on the shore and fled before the British search party arrived.

Penny was captured by the British on Sunday night, August 21, 1813, and taken from his home on Three Mile Harbor wearing only his nightshirt. He was taken to Halifax prison, where he stayed for nine months until he was returned under a prisoner exchange by President James Madison. He received a hero's welcome and, with the help of his friend Jeremiah Osborn, he published a book of his adventures in 1815, entitled, *The Life and Adventures of Joshua Penny: Interspersed With Many Curious Incidents and Hair Breadth Escapes.*

In 1823, East Hampton Town declared "that Joshua Penny be allowed the use and privilege of the sedge which he set out on the flat, near the mouth of Three Mile Harbor, during his residence in this town." *Sedge* is a grass with a triangular stem, which grows in wetlands. Sedge Island in front of his house overlooking Three Mile Harbor was renamed Penny Sedge Island. He was given permission by the Town to build a wharf at the landing place near his house at Squaw Cove. The road paralleling the east side of the Harbor was called

Clockwise From Top Left: Captain John Foulkes Hussey steering his boat, the A.V.H., out of the Harbor • Anna V. Hussey with friend's child • Friends on the A.V.H. in Three Mile Harbor • The Husseys' house on the shores of Three Mile Harbor, with Penny Sedge Island in background

Penny's Highway by the townspeople in his honor. The road name has since been changed to Three Mile Harbor Road Hog Creek Highway.

In 1834, Penny married Molly Gann, the sister of his good friend. He enjoyed only six years of marriage before he died in 1840 at the age of 67. His cemetery is still near the shores of Three Mile Harbor on Roosevelt Avenue. A neighbor's wife, Mary Bennet (Bennett), is also buried there. She had been married to Edward 5th Bennett, a soldier in the Revolution, who served with Captain Ezekiel Mulford's Company, Colonel Josiah Smith's Regiment, and also the 1st Regiment, Suffolk County Minute Men. Edward Bennett's father was a soldier in the French and Indian War.

George Washington Gann lived south of Joshua Penny's house at the foot of Gann Road. Born in 1827, he was an independent and feisty man who lived to be 102. In his youth, George Washington Gann was serving on Captain George Hand's ship in the Pacific when the boat started to sink. The crew was ordered to continually man the pumps, but Gann, being exhausted beyond limit, refused to obey the order. He was strung up by his thumbs, to serve as an example to the crew, who were also ready to rebel. After seeing how Gann was punished, the crew decided not to rebel.

Gann's nickname with the locals was the "Clammin' Man." After he had gathered about 50 to 100 bushels of clams in Three Mile Harbor, he would sail his boat,

The Comet, to Connecticut to sell them. People sang this ditty about him: *George Gann, a clammin' man Washed his face in a fryin' pan Combed his hair by the light of the moon Brushed his teeth with a rusty spoon*

A story is told that a friend came to his house one morning to go eeling. George wanted to have breakfast quickly, so he drank some pancake batter without cooking it, saying, "All goes to the same place. No difference if I cook it or not."

There were other Ganns who went whaling between 1812 and 1940, never to return. They were Daniel, George, John, Jr., and William. There are no more Ganns left in East Hampton.

After Joshua Penny passed away, Captain John Foulkes Hussey, his wife, Anna V. Chapman, and her six-year-old half brother, Robert Smith, moved into the old Penny house in 1888.

Hussey, born on January 29, 1856, in Staffordshire, England, ran away from home at an early age. His mother died when he was young, and, not wanting to go to school, he was lured by the excitement of life at sea. Starting as a cabin boy on a square-rigger at the age of ten, he traveled to the Mediterranean, the coast of Africa, Scandinavia, the Caribbean, China, and America. He was granted a master's license in Hong Kong in 1884, which gave him "Unlimited Papers" and the command of any size

ship. After commanding a Japanese gunboat in the China Sea and noticing how well-armed they were, he predicted, "Mark my words, someday we'll have trouble with the Japanese."

He met the woman who became his wife in New London. While he was at sea in the British West Indies, she gave birth to twins, but both died before he got home. As a result of her pleading, he settled down in Three Mile Harbor in 1888 and started a clamming and fishing business. He would sail his catch to New London and return with kerosene, flour, and other supplies. In 1894, he built a new sloop yacht, the *A.V.H.*, named after his wife's initials. He chartered moonlight sails that were enhanced by his colorful sea stories. The sloop was outfitted with a gasoline engine in 1904 so he could get his clams to Connecticut as soon as possible.

Hussey was tough, ornery, stubborn, and also hand-icapped by extreme deafness and the loss of one eye. Once Hussey's boat was blocking the channel and another fisherman, Henry Luce, could not get his boat out of the Harbor. Luce asked him to move his boat, but Hussey wouldn't, so Luce cut Hussey's lines. Luce had to pay a fine in court for his actions and was not a happy fisherman!

Hussey constantly feuded with his neighbor to the north, Gardner Peckham. When Peckham was found dead on a cold January morning in 1905, Hussey, being a prime suspect, was arrested. J.T. Gardiner paid his $1,000 bond and had him released. No proof was ever found that Hussey was involved in his neighbor's death. Although he was tough, he was very moral and prayed daily with his wife when she was dying. After sixty years of marriage, she passed away in 1947. He moved to Amagansett the next year, and in April 1950, Captain Hussey died at the age of 94.

Francis Ray Smith, Hussey's step-grandson, related the following story before his death in July 2001. While Hussey was in New London, with his boat tied up at the dock, there was a gang nearby raising Cain. One of the fellows spit on Hussey's deck. Hussey yelled, "You do that again, and you'll clean my deck!" The fellow did it again. The two of them fought it out, until the rabble-rouser finally gave up, saying, "That was a good go-round, let's have a drink together!" So Hussey had a drink with John L. Sullivan, the champion fighter.

It would be interesting to research the genealogy of John Foulkes Hussey! Husseys were known as a sea-people, according to a Southampton Hussey. The name is also mentioned in *The New York Times* bestseller *In the Heart of the Sea*, by Nathaniel Philbrick, the history of the sinking of the whale ship *Essex*. The founder of Macy's department store, Roland Hussey Macy, came from Ireland. 🐚

Rumrunning

*R*umrunning was quite active in Three Mile Harbor, although some would deny it. In the United States, Prohibition went into effect with the Eighteenth Amendment on July 16, 1920, and lasted until it was repealed in December 1933. Wholesale liquor was brought in from Canada and the West Indies by ships that would anchor outside the 12-mile legal boundary, forming what was called Rum Row. "Rumrunners" would bring the bootleg liquor ashore, trying to evade the Coast Guard and the feds.

Exerpt from
"The Smugglers' Chanty"
by Joseph Chase Allen, 1921

"Oh, we don't give a damn for 'our old Uncle Sam
Way-o, whisky and gin!
Lend us a hand when we stand in to land
Just give us time to run the rum in."

...Unto our unprotected shores
Forbidden rum they bring
Patrol boats chase them by the scores
But still the pirates sing:

"Oh, schooners and steamers and cruisers and all
Way-o, whisky and gin!
Chase us with cutters and battleships tall
Still we have time to bring the rum in."

...Our laws are dry as dry can be
Although the land is moist
And jolly pirates out at sea
Chant loudly as they hoist:

"'Tis easy and free for us boys out at sea
Way-o, whisky and gin!
Pigs will all fly when the country goes dry
Give us the word, we'll run the rum in."

During Prohibition, the boats doing rumrunning needed frequent repairs because they ran at night and ran fast. Wessberg's Boat Yard at the Head of the Harbor would haul them out only at night, under the cover of darkness. John Warren, an employee at the boatyard during those years, chuckled while remembering the following incidents.

The *Desiree*, a rumrunner owned by Charlie Walker and Joe Mochelle, needed a quick repair one night because the whole stern of the boat had been wrenched out when they had tried to make a fast escape. Unfortunately, they forgot that the boat was still tied up at anchor when they took off.

Their other boat, the *Bernadeen*, would carry liquor down in the hold while people danced to music on the top deck to give the appearance of propriety. The feds never suspected them of rumrunning, and they went right by the Coast Guard without a search. When Prohibition ended, the *Bernadeen* had a "mysterious" fire while it was blocked on land at Wessberg's. Although there was smoke, there was little fire. The wood was a hard mahogany, so it just smoldered and wouldn't burn up. It was surmised that the owners were trying to get rid of it, because kerosene cans were found in the bushes not far away.

Emerson Taber brought liquor to shore in his speedboat and stored it in his garage on David's Lane until he could ship it to New York City. One night, he lost a whole shipment because his driver unloaded the liquor in a neighbor's garage by mistake. The neighbor, Casper Rowe, being a teetotaler, promptly turned over the liquor to the federal authorities.

Another story relates how Emerson Taber was helped by a local undertaker, who would use his hearse to cart the "goods" undetected to New York City. Taber's wife would even drive the hearse, to further the deception. After the repeal of Prohibition, Emerson Taber moved to Gann Road and opened Taber's Lobsters on the Commercial Dock.

Edward M. Osborne, who lived on the eastern shores of Three Mile Harbor, recalled how his neighbor Budd King had his own boat ramp built next to his house north of Shagwong Marina so his boat the *Helen*, captained by Tom Rose, could unload the liquor into trucks and drive off easily. He also had a subbasement under his house to store liquor until it could be delivered. Budd unfortunately had his income drastically cut when Prohibition ended, and he had to give up his house. Ed Osborne bought Budd King's house for $12,000 to help him out.

Victor Kliesrath owned another rumrunner of the twenties called *Yap-Yap* (pay-pay backward). Fortunes were made and lost easily in those years. Many locals were caught up in these dangerous shipments, with some stories of murders, gang warfare, and so on still waiting to be told.

Innocent people also became involved. Jarvis Wood didn't have a boat, but he was standing in shallow water clamming when his rake hit a box filled with liquor. Not being a drinker, he sold it and bought a new car with the money. Many people here profited by Prohibition, but there were also a lot of people who believed that liquor was an evil to society. 🌿

Above: View of Three Mile Harbor Boatyard. Boats left to right are Skippy, *later called* Splinter, *Emerson Taber's lobster boat, and at far right is the burned hull of the* Bernadeen, *a rumrunner owned by Charlie Walker and Joe Mochelle. (Photo courtesy of C.E. King)*
Facing Page: "Smuggler's Chanty," from The Black Ships, *by Everett Allen, published by Little, Brown and Company. ● Rumrunner dumping the evidence while being chased by the feds (Illustration by Scott Hewett)*

Early Industry

*T*he sustenance of the townspeople was mainly from the land and the sea. Given the choice, the early settlers would rather have worked on the land. Landownership was the key to status and wealth. Fishing required equipment, salt for curing, and an investor to supply the money. Investors from Massachusetts, who were backed by investors from London, were able to supply salt codfish, whale oil, timber, and farm produce to the tropical colonies and southern Europe. East Hampton settlers, though, needed first to take care of their land investments, and they worked very hard at clearing, planting, raising cattle, building homes, and self-protection. They needed to attract artisans like millers, weavers, and blacksmiths. In order to discourage transient laborers, anyone hired in the town had to stay for a minimum of three years.

Land had already been stripped of trees by the Indians, creating meadows for grazing livestock. The townspeople's livestock were herded together and taken up Main Street to common pastures for grazing. Ocean Avenue was once called Calf Pasture Lane. This was a private grazing land, barred by a fence across the road. The areas set apart for grazing "in common" were meadows in areas now known as Accabonac Harbor, Maidstone Park, and Clearwater. Salt marsh hay (Spartina grass) was harvested near the shores of Three Mile Harbor and Accabonac Harbor. It was highly prized, providing fodder for the cattle and sheep in the winter. At low tide in Three Mile Harbor, horses fitted with wooden platform shoes (so they wouldn't sink in the mud) would pull a cart over to Penny Sedge Island or to Goose Island (Dayton's or Keyes' Island). The grass was cut, loaded on the cart, and carried back before the tide came in.

According to Trustee Records, in 1866 the Sedge Flats at Three Mile Harbor and at Accabonac Harbor were hired out for mowing as often as the Town Trustees could "dispose of the privilege," thus establishing ownership in the town and bringing a small revenue to the Trustees.

Seaweed was accessible and useful. It was harvested at low tides from the beach, baled, and shipped to New York City to be used for insulation and fire-proofing. The local houses had their foundations banked with seaweed for insulation in the winter. Seaweed was also used in the hog pens for bedding. Ice was kept frozen for summer use by packing it in seaweed. It was an invaluable commodity!

Leather tanning was a very important industry here. In 1775, there were 2,000 cattle and 4,000 sheep grazing in Montauk, providing hides. The dreens (streams) at the southern end of Three Mile Harbor were used to tan the leather in the oak-bark-drenched waters. Soak Hides Dreen still has these tannin-rich waters next to the road by the Head of the Harbor. Vats for soaking the leather were a common sight along Three Mile Harbor Road. Since Lynn, Massachusetts, had an important shoemaking industry, there was a market nearby. Thousands of people were employed as "cordwainers" or leather workers in Lynn. Many farmers took care of their fields in the summer and made shoes in the winter.

The Hedges family, with its large herd of cattle, had a tanning facility that produced leather for the shoemakers. Stephen Hedges's son John and grandson Daniel supplied shoes to markets across the Sound as well as locally.

Above: Harvesting hay (From the collection of Sylvia Mendelman)
Right: Horses were fitted with these wooden shoes to prevent their sinking in the mud when carting sedge grass off Penny Sedge Island or Dayton's Island. (Courtesy of East Hampton Town Marine Museum in Amagansett. East Hampton Historical Society)

 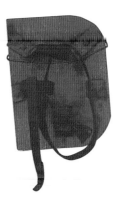

Above: *Feeding chickens on the Hussey property (From the collection of Mary Fitzgerald)*
Facing Page
Top: *Cows on Main Street, East Hampton (Courtesy of C. Frank Dayton Collection, East Hampton Library)*
Bottom: *Lop trees can be seen throughout the area. Lopping was the fencing of choice for East Hampton settlers. It spared the trees and cost nothing. (Illustration by Marvin Kuhn)*

the man replied, "Today I'm alive and well, but I might die (dye) tomorrow."

The use of wood was very restricted. In 1676, a license was needed to cut wood in East Hampton. Small trees were "lopped" to create fences cheaply without killing the trees. In March, when the sap started to run, a cut was made on one side of the tree and then the tree was pulled over horizontally, creating a boundary fence when branches filled in. George Washington, on an inspection of the village, did not think much of the method because they couldn't fence in the hogs properly. Lopping, though, was the fencing of choice for East Hampton settlers. It spared the trees and cost nothing. There are still some old lopped trees throughout the area.

Wool was another valuable local commodity in East Hampton. Gardiner's Island had thousands of sheep. After the sheep were sheared, the wool was taken to the shore for shipment to East Hampton. The island and the mainland would signal each other from the shore with smoke fires made with seaweed when pickups were needed. Springs-Fireplace is so named for this custom. The triangle on Gay Lane in the village was the site of the old sheepfold, or pen. When some of the wool was combined with flax, it was called linsey-woolsey, a popular cloth for clothing. Flax was harvested by carefully pulling out the plant so that its long fibers were preserved.

Linen, made from flax, was used to make cloth, thread, bedding, sails, and seining nets. Early settlers had no cotton available for fabric — just linen, wool, linsey-woolsey, and leather.

Abigail Edwards Field, of the Franklin Farm, told this amusing story about a Mr. Babcock who took his cloth to a man to dye it. He came back two weeks later, but the dye job was not finished yet. When he asked the man when it would be finished,

Cordwood and lumber did not become an important industry until the mid-1700s. Large trees for timber were scarce when the settlers first came to East Hampton. Indians had practiced annual burnings in early spring to clear the land for planting and to increase the meadowland for deer hunting.

The wood for the second church built in East Hampton in 1717 was brought over from Gardiner's Island, where the trees were not subjected to annual burnings and had grown very tall. They were highly prized for use in construction. One of the trees on Gardiner's Island in 1838 measured 17 feet in circumference. A white oak cut in 1836 measured 6 feet in diameter.

Moving wooden houses instead of building new ones was a common practice. Houses were easily carted to the new site on rollers. Many of the early settlers' homes were built using prefabricated wooden homes made in New England and shipped from Boston, to be assembled once they arrived.

By 1736, the wood resources here increased and became a source of fuel for Boston and New York City. The wood was cut from the shores of the harbors and bays and shipped out by boat, easing the transportation problems of hauling wood overland.

The difficulties of transportation restricted industry from seeking markets far away. The townspeople tried to take care of their needs from the resources they had at hand. Neighbors helped each other, and a barter system of trade flourished locally,

Lop Tree   M. Kuhn

The sandy soil of Springs was excellent for raising poultry, so the raising of chickens, ducks, and geese became a large industry. Nothing went to waste in this industry. The poultry could be killed and prepared quickly when needed for dinner, eliminating the need for refrigeration. Eggs were plentiful, feathers were used for bedding, and droppings made good fertilizer. The Miller farm on Fireplace Road near Accabonac Harbor was a popular poultry and egg supplier. The Hodder Poultry Store was located near Maidstone Park, where Michael's Restaurant stands today. 🍂

Above: Rendering blubber into oil was time-consuming. A whale's blubber was chopped into small pieces and then heated in large caldrons, melting it into oil. (Photo courtesy of the East Hampton Historical Society)
Right: Beached whale, photo taken in the 1890s (Photo courtesy of the East Hampton Historical Society)

Whaling, an important industry, was already well established in the sixteenth and seventeenth centuries by the English, French, Dutch, and Norwegians. East Hampton first carried on whaling from the shore by harvesting beached right whales. In 1664, there were four "wards" established along the beach to watch for stranded whales. When whales were found, they were divided up amongst the townspeople. The Indians got the fins, and the townspeople got the blubber, rendering it into oil in huge caldrons right on the beach. The whale oil was used for heat, light, and as a lubricant. The flexible baleen was used for corset stays.

The years 1830 to 1860 were the peak of the whaling industry. Fortunes could be made if there were successful voyages. More than 60 ships sailed from Sag Harbor for the purpose of whaling. Whale oil was rendered from blubber right on the ship when a catch was made. Captain Jonathan Osborne (1771–1856) was a well-known whaler and a large landowner. His responsibilities shifted between his fields and his ship. One day, after sailing out of Sag Harbor, he took the ship down to Hedges Banks and ordered the anchor dropped. Then, he said, "This is now my ship. I hold her papers, and no one can give orders but myself. I have a field of corn home that needs cutting, and I am going home to have it done, and will be back later." He left his crew on the ship, went home, and returned after harvesting his corn — something shocking for the captain of a ship!

The industry diminished after 1860 because of two major events. First, the Gold Rush of the 1840s lured fortune hunters to California. Ships were crewed with young men from East Hampton who signed up for dreams of riches but, unfortunately, never realized their dreams and never returned home. Second, petroleum soon replaced whale oil as fuel. Whale oil was no longer in high demand. Without markets, the industry floundered. By 1871, the last whaling ship had sailed from Sag Harbor. 🐚

R.C. Emery

Finfishing and Shellfishing

Fishing, if I, a fisher, may protest.

Of pleasures is the sweetest, of sports the best,

Of exercises the most excellent,

Of recreations the most innocent.

But now the sport is marred, and wot ye why?

Fishes decrease, and fishers multiply.

—John Weever

The gathering of small fish, clams, eels, scallops, and oysters helped supplement incomes in East Hampton and put food on the table for many. Rarely, though, did anyone of means remain a fisherman by choice. Income was not steady and required the investment of equipment. In 1675, there were only about a dozen fishing "shallops," or small boats. Since the boats had to be hauled up on shore by hand, they had to be small. By 1725, there were many commercial fishermen using ketches and schooners, some two-masted and up to 65 feet long, sailing along the coast from Massachusetts to the Caribbean. Dockage for these large ships and whalers was mainly at Sag Harbor. Along the shore, the catch had to be filleted and dried by spreading the fillet out skin side down on slats or bark, after which salt was poured on the flesh. To prevent dew or rain from spoiling the curing overnight, the fish had to be turned over, skin side up, every night. If a crew member who had been drinking a bit too much in the evening forgot to turn the fish before he went to bed, the whole catch was ruined by morning!

There was a great need for salt cod in Barbados and the other slave-trading states. Merchant ships supplied this need and in return brought back salt, sugar, spices, tobacco, cotton, and slaves. The merchant industry was paralyzed by the Revolutionary War because most of the ships were destroyed. After the War of 1812, the merchant fishing industry ended, yet there was still a big demand for fish because a domestic market began to thrive. Delivery was still a problem, though. Catches had to be delivered to nearby markets due to lack of refrigeration. Smaller boats filled the need because they could both catch the fish and deliver it quickly.

Locally, fishing was done with net traps (pound traps) attached to poles set near shore, using small boats. The net was drawn up and the fish were scooped into the boats. Another method was to wade out with two people holding the ends of the net and dragging the net to shore. In the more efficient "haul-seining" method, boats with nets were taken out through the waves and a horse on shore pulled the net in to shore. Horses were replaced by trucks in the twentieth century.

Most of the local fish have their "run," or season when they are abundant, such as bluefish, striped bass, cod, weakfish, fluke, flounder, porgy, blackfish, and pollock. "Weakfish come when the lilacs bloom" is some old sage advice, as is, "When the shad bush blooms, the shad fish comes."

Alewife herring leave the bay in early spring on a high tide to spawn upstream and then return to the sea or bay. Gathering these fish also depended on the time of year.

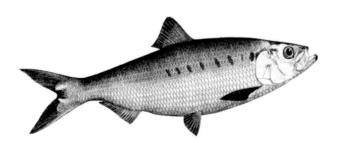

Above: Hickory Shadfish
Facing Page: Pound-trap hauling, early 1900s (Photos courtesy of Isabel Gardiner Mairs)

Weakfish

Cod

Porgy

Striped Bass

Blackfish

Flounder

Bluefish

Fluke (Summer Flounder)

Clams were raked from the shallow flats using hand rakes and tongs. Although oysters and scallops were abundant, they were not appreciated in the early years and were used mostly for livestock and fertilizer. The twentieth century brought the fame of "Springs Escallops" and oysters to the nation when they were served in the finest restaurants of New York City.

The flats in Three Mile Harbor and Accabonac Harbor had the best clams, oysters, and scallops. Harry Field owned a scallop house at the Head of the Harbor, where Gardiner's Marina is today. His father, Samuel B. Field, was a whaleman. Harry taught the harvesting and marketing of scallops to his son, Harvey, who liked to "test" the scallops a little earlier than the legal season. He would get a few before the season opened from Eli's Channel on the west side of the Harbor. Maybe he just wanted to be sure he'd get the chance to taste a few. His wife, Rita, had a small ranch behind their house, which she called the Rocking Horse Ranch. Harvey played western-style music for local affairs and was a well-liked fellow.

Refrigeration of the catch was a big problem. Ice had to be harvested in the winter and stored for summer's use. When the ice was thick, horse-driven saws cut out chunks of ice, which were dragged to an icehouse that was submerged underground and then covered with seaweed or straw for insulation. There was an icehouse near Duck Creek and also by Ashawagh Hall at Mary Louise Dodge's house. The ice was used primarily by the fishermen in the summer to keep their catch fresh. The luxury of ice for anything except cooling fish was unthinkable.

Other perishable foods were usually kept in root cellars — simple holes dug in the ground and covered over with wood. The cellars, or "barnes," kept the food from freezing in the winter and kept it cool in the summer. Some of the early settlers were annoyed that the Indians who dug these barnes for their provisions would eventually abandon them uncovered and the settlers' livestock would fall into them.

Above Left to Right: Fulton Fish Market (Photo courtesy of East Hampton Historical Society) • Postcard depicting Tonging and the shellfish industry (Photo courtesy of East Hampton Historical Society) • Frederick Parker Lester raking clams (Photo courtesy of Gayle D. Lester)

A well was another cool spot in the summer to keep perishables like butter and milk. Early wells were simple cisterns made by hollowing out a large tree trunk and setting it over the springs bubbling out of the ground. The water was always cool and fresh. There was one such cistern at the Head of Three Mile Harbor near the Town Dock.

There were few options for delivering fresh fish to the markets. One was by water. Boats would come in to Three Mile Harbor from Connecticut to pick up catches. They would come right up to the clammer in the water and take his catch on a regular basis. The other option was by horse-drawn carts, which delivered the fish to Amagansett, Riverhead, and Sag Harbor. The trip from Three Mile Harbor to Sag Harbor took eight hours round trip on the East Hampton Turnpike (Route 114), and wagons had to pay a toll of three cents each way. The toll booth was located on Route 114 near Lincoln Road, but it has since burned down. It wasn't until 1895 that the train came to Sag Harbor and Montauk, enabling delivery of the catch to the Fulton Fish Market in New York City and thereby increasing the market for seafood.

Oysters were abundant in the brackish coastal waters along the Atlantic coast. By 1836, three hundred boats dredged for oysters in Long Island Sound alone. After 1910, overfishing in Maryland and pollution from manmade chemicals in Connecticut led to the decline of oyster beds there, so Long Island oysters increased in value 100 percent. Bottom-land leases were given to D. J. Gardiner in Three Mile Harbor for five dollars per year. In 1909, when S. C. Grimshaw applied for a lease, it was denied, possibly because he ran a large operation on the North Fork and locals wanted to protect their resource.

The Reich Brothers, a fish distributor from Patchogue, started to make daily pickups by truck in 1910, increasing the market availability for the fishermen. The economic advantages of fishing soon lured many farmers in East Hampton to a life on the water.

When Fishermen Meet

(Courtesy Mr. and Mrs. Clarence E. King)

"Hiyamac"

"Lobuddy"

"Binearlong"

"Coplours"

"Cetchanenny"

"Goddafew"

"Kindarthay"

"Bassencarp"

"Ennysizetoom"

"Cuplapowns"

"Sordalike"

"Wahchoozin?"

"Gobbawurms"

"Fishanonaboddum"

"Rydononaboddum"

"Whatchadrinkin?"

"Jugajimbeam"

"Igoddago"

"Tubad"

"Seeyaroun"

"Yeatakidezzy"

"Guluk."

Facing page: Clammer V. Jarvis Wood (This photograph was taken by John Chao in 1983, commissioned by Adelaide de Menil.)
Above Left: Sprig Gardner, the champion wrestling coach for East Hampton High School, is about to fillet his striped bass. His fishing buddy was Doc Fish, and they knew how to catch them! Sprig lived on Gallatin Road in a house that had stored liquor for rumrunners in the 1920s. (Photo taken in the 1970s by Sylvia Mendelman)
Above Right and Below: Ralph George was the only Marine Patrolman for the Town of East Hampton from 1969 to 1984. (Photos courtesy of Ralph George)

Clams were guarded jealously here. They were prized for their medicinal properties as well as for their taste and nutrition. In 1861, a nonresident of East Hampton was jailed in Riverhead for taking clams out of Three Mile Harbor.

A Springs fisherman, Jarvis Wood, fished with his father on a 30-foot boat and also clammed in Three Mile Harbor. Once when he went clamming on Penny Sedge Island, old Captain Hussey chased him away, saying that those were *his* clams. Jarvis remembered that the best clamming places were on the flats behind Dayton's Island and the Duck Creek flats. He said, "The soft clams were the best. In an hour or so, you could fill a bushel with 'em."

The fall of 1932 had a brown tide. This detrimental algae bloom killed most of the seaweed in the Harbor. Scallops did not set due to lack of oxygen. An analysis by the City of New Rochelle found that an iodine excrescence from a certain type of seaweed occurs every twenty years, and 1932 was the twentieth year. In 1985, the brown tide appeared again and killed shellfish once more. Scientists are still researching the cause of this plague of our waters, but they have not been able to determine why the tide appears.

In 1932, the Trustees adopted an ordinance forbidding nonresidents from taking scallops or clams from Town waters. Residents were restricted to taking fish and shellfish from Town waters only by hand-powered dredges (commercial fishermen exempt) between sunrise and sunset. The scallops had to be more than two inches across. The season for taking scallops was from September 1 to March 30. The season for clams was from October 1 to May 31.

The Trustees then hired a patrolman to enforce shellfish laws in 1936. The Bay patrolman placed five million flounder fry (young fish) in Town waters. New ordinances were drafted. Beam trawls could not be used in Town waters. Starfish could not be thrown back in the water. Seed oysters and shellfish could not be taken from restricted areas. No scallops could be taken from February 1 to October 1. Trash could not be dumped in the water. No fences, docks, or buoys could go in the water without permission.

The destructive starfish infestation of Three Mile Harbor in 1940 was a concern of Bay Constable Elmer Daniels. Suggestions were made to use widgeon grass and lime to kill them. The Trustees

Two hundred fifty bushels of seed oysters were purchased from L. H. Molloy at $2.25 a bushel and planted in the water by Elmer Daniels. Fanny Gardiner was in charge of a project to build devices to cover and protect shellfish during the spawning season. East Hampton is still trying to protect and replenish this industry today with its Aquaculture Program and legislation.

The lobster industry has also had its problems. The summer of 1998 had a die-off disaster in the western part of Long Island Sound that was thought to be caused by two factors: one, the spraying of malathion for mosquito control in Connecticut, and two, shell rot caused by a parasite. This combination reduced the harvest by 60 percent along Long Island Sound. Here on the East End, the lobster harvest was under by 40 percent in 2000.

The decline of lobsters has resulted in size restrictions being placed on commercial fishermen. They have been forbidden to take females with eggs and females with a V notch in their tails (egg-bearing lobsters). The federal government currently has a relief program for the lobstermen to tide them over during this disaster.

Commercial fishermen share the excellent fishing grounds between the north and south forks of Long Island with recreational sport fishermen.

Dudley Roberts, an avid sports fisherman, docked his boat the *Malia* at the Harbor Marina back in the fifties and sixties, when Jim Taylor ran it. Dudley was part of a camaraderie of other fishermen that included Doc Fish, Lou Seitz, Sprig Gardner, and Chick Phillips.

Charles H. (Chick) Phillips kept his boat at Shagwong Marina. He knew the fishing spots around Gardiner's Bay better than anybody. His biggest problem was what to do with all the fish he caught. He said his secret to fishing was getting the right tools (boat, rods, lures, bait) and learning how to use them. He'd get up at 4 A.M. every day, drive down to Newtown Lane for coffee and the "news," and then fish for the day. This was his well-deserved retirement routine after owning Chick Phillips Garage in the village for years.

His boat, *Chick-a-D,* became his motivating force when he was struggling with Lou Gehrig's disease. His leg muscles withered away, but he still fished on his boat. Friends would cart him in a wheelbarrow to the bulkhead, where he had rigged up a sling with a pulley so he could get on his boat by himself.

ordered two tons of "stardust" (Granular Q Lime, manufactured by the North East Company in Adams, Massachusetts) to be dumped in the water. The lime produced an ulcer on the starfish and killed them. They also dumped three floats of jingle shells on the bottom of the Harbor to protect seed oysters from these predators.

A night watchman was hired in 1941 to protect the "escallops" from poachers. Then, in 1942, a law was passed prohibiting dredging for shellfish with a sailboat; only hand-powered boats were allowed for dredging.

Unfortunately, the winter of 1943 was very stormy and cold, and many clams were lost. People in Town were worried about the scarcity of shellfish. The Fish and Wildlife Service presented a talk on the damage done to shellfish by herring gulls. Jarvis Wood suggested taking the dry scallop shells from the dump and returning them to the water so the scallop bugs could set on them, but no action was ever taken.

In the 1950s, a second night watchman was hired to protect the scallops from poachers. The Trustees passed a resolution forbidding dredging and bull raking at the Head of the Harbor, but rescinded it one month later following a petition from the fishermen. They tried to increase the resources by buying spawn for soft-shell clams and seed oysters.

Top: The dragger Saint Anthony, *owned by Pat Malik, returning to the Harbor after a day of fishing (Photo by Randy Handwerger)*

Middle: Chick-a-D, *a 28-foot Uniflite Salty Dog, and her captain, Charles H. Phillips (Chick), in 1973. (Photo courtesy of Dot Phillips)*

Bottom: The Malia, *with Dudley Roberts of East Hampton at the helm, heading out to a good fishing spot (From the David Edwardes collection)*

Facing Page

Top: Commercial lobster boat silhouetted by the sunset at the Commercial Dock (Photo by Mark Mendelman)

Bottom: Lobster pots stacked at the Commercial Dock (Photo by Diane C. Hewett)

Wild Foods and Herbs

*T*he settlers found the area around Three Mile Harbor excellent hunting grounds for all sorts of wildlife. There was an abundance of ducks, geese, pheasant, and other wild foul, along with deer, raccoon, squirrel, and other game. The natural seepage of fresh springs provided drinking water, good ground cover for habitat, and lush vegetation for food.

Above: Duck hunters (Photo courtesy of East Hampton Historical Society)
Facing Page
Top: *Beach plum blossoms at Maidstone Park in the spring (Photo by Diane C. Hewett) The beach plums growing at Maidstone Park are gathered each fall by local jam makers, keeping a watchful eye for poison ivy and ticks. The jam is a specialty of this area, and picking the fruit is a late-summer tradition.*
Bottom: *Frederick Parker Lester (Pops) picking beach plums in late summer, and "Pops" with his son Frederick William, posing with buckets of picked plums (Photos courtesy of Gayle D. Lester)*

The shores around the Harbor provided an abundance of wild berries, beach plums, grapes, cranberries, rose hips, blueberries, raspberries, strawberries, blackberries, nuts, and fruit trees. The larder could be well stocked with preserves for winter.

The Indians ate "ground nuts," or potatoes *(Apios tuberosa),* which they dug up and boiled into a soup. Some early settlers tried eating these ground nuts but disliked them, saying they tasted like liver. Other wild foods gathered in the fields were wild carrots, leeks, fiddlehead ferns, lettuce, and grains. Medicine was obtained from plants that grew in abundance, such as the bark of the willow tree, which relieved pain, and a tea made from sassafras roots. The bark was used to treat fever and as a general tonic for gas. (*Note:* It has been found to be a carcinogen.) The native white pine was also supposed to have healing powers. Indians thought the white pine could cure ills by simply leaning against it and breathing in its aroma.

The settlers soon learned to use such wild herbs as bearberry, purslane, sour grass, joe-pye weed, witch hazel, lady's slipper, and others. The Indians were ritualistic when picking herbs, calling out, "Mother Earth, I am reaching into your side for this herb" and repeating the name of the herb three times.

Bayberry, which made fragrant candles, was in such demand that a law was passed in 1772 that would allow the gathering of the berries only after September 20. Common candles were made from beef tallow, but the special, fine-grade candles made from bayberry could be sold for extra income in the winter. Bay leaves were used in cooking, and bayberry branches helped repel mosquitoes.

Sweet flag *(Acorus callamus)* grew in moist areas. In addition to using the aromatic leaves to add fragrance to stuffy rooms, a tea made from the rhizome was used for indigestion, fevers, and as a stimulant. Sweet flag should not be confused with blue flag *(Iris versicolor* and *Iris prismatica),* whose flower is similar to the European yellow flag.

Indians used blue flag in a poultice for treating bruises and sores. The rhizome is poisonous, although the Indians used it to treat liver ailments, rheumatism, and syphilis. Blue flag is also named poison flag and water flag. It grew in abundance at the end of Flaggy Hole Road.

Blue Flag

6165   OLD FIELDS HOUSE. THREE MILE HARBOR, L. I.   PUBL. BY W. J. HOPPER, EAST HAMPTON, L, I.

Zebulon Pike Montgomery Field ("Uncle Zeb") lived in a tiny house by the Head of Three Mile Harbor from 1831 to 1906. Every day, he walked to the village peddling sweet flag, wintergreen, and sweet cicely. Sweet cicely *(Myrrhis odorata)* is an anise-scented plant useful for seasoning cooked fruits. The seeds can also be used to polish and scent wooden furniture. Zeb liked to sing hymns as he walked, his favorite being "Put on a Long White Robe Like Job and Sail Away to Galilee." People wondered why his house was painted only halfway up, but that was his way. He only painted his house as far as he could reach. In 1959, the house was bought by Thomas Miller, but it has since been demolished.

Wild foods were supplemented by planting and cultivating squash, corn, and beans. Beans were planted around the corn stalk, thereby utilizing a natural support for the bean vines. Crops were fertilized by burying an oily fish (menhaden, or bunker) in each corn hill. Corn was eaten almost

every day by the Indians and early settlers. Cracked corn boiled in water was their daily porridge, called samp. On Sundays, cooking was not allowed, since it was the day of worship and rest, so samp was cooked on Saturday and kept warm on the back of the stove for Sunday's dinner.

Wheat, rye, oats, and other grains were also cultivated. The local miller ground the grain into flour. Mills were powered in different ways—by water, horses, or the wind. Because East Hampton had no streams to dam for water power, the early settlers were granted the privilege of bringing their grain to Water Mill as long as they helped dig out the "sea-poose" there. This was a narrow opening to the sea, which created a tremendous rush of water with the tides. In East Hampton, they used both a horse-driven mill and windmills. Joshua Garelick, who lived at Three Mile Harbor, was one of the first millers for East Hampton.

Facing Page Top: *Postcard of Uncle Zeb standing next to his house, located just north of the Bennett cemetery at the Head of Three Mile Harbor (Postcard from the Harvey Ginsberg Collection at East Hampton Library)*

Facing Page Bottom: *Sweet cicely, a sweet herb that tastes like fennel*

Above, Left Top: *Prickly pear cactus is actually an edible plant with many medicinal uses. (Photo by Sylvia Mendelman)*

Above, Left Bottom: *Rosa rugosa, hardy and abundant along the sandy shoreline, has flowers that last until fall, when a red "hip" develops, which can be harvested for jam or tea. (Photo by Diane C. Hewett)*

Above, Right: *Chicory (Chichorium) "blue sailors" has edible leaves nutritionally high in calcium, potassium, and vitamins A and C. The root can be slow-roasted and ground into a coffee substitute. (Photo by Diane C. Hewett)*

Local Recipes

*S*ome are old, Some are for blues,
Some are borrowed,
Some are new.

Above: Pierre Franey serving his famous "Moules Marinière" at the Springs Improvement Society Fisherman's Fair, August 1979 (Photo by Cal Norris, courtesy of The East Hampton Star)

Pierre Franey's Moules Marinière

Combine in a large pot and simmer for
3 minutes: 1 cup dry white wine
         3 chopped shallots
         1/2 bay leaf
         1/2 tsp. thyme
         black pepper
         4 sprigs parsley
         3 tbsp. butter

Add 3 pounds scrubbed and debearded mussels.

Cover and cook over high heat for 5 to 10 minutes, until the mussels are opened. Shake pot occasionally while cooking to redistribute mussels so they will cook evenly.

Spoon mussels and broth into bowls, sprinkle with chopped parsley, and serve with hot, buttered French bread rubbed with garlic.

Serves 4.

The late Pierre Franey lived in Springs and authored many gourmet cookbooks. His moules and crepes were favorite foods at the Fishermen's Fair at Ashawagh Hall each August. Pierre's son, Jacques, now owns and runs a wine shop in Springs carrying on family traditions of good food and wine.

Bonac Clam Pie

Saute 1/2 cup chopped onions. When cooked, add 3 cups ground, drained clams, 3/4 cup unsalted, crumbled crackers, and 3/4 cup evaporated milk. Grind pepper on top. Parsley or bacon may be added to the filling. Pour into a pie shell, and cover with a top shell. Prick crust with a fork, and bake in a 375° oven for 45 minutes or until browned.

Aromatic Grilled Fish

- Fillet your fish with skin and scales left on. Wash and pat dry.
- Place fish on aluminum foil, skin side down.
- Sprinkle fillets with a salad dressing of your choice.
- Thinly slice red onions, red peppers, and garlic (optional). Spread over the fillet.
- Gather some wild grape vines, strip off the leaves, and wad the vines into a bundle. *Note:* Apple branches or mesquite may be used if you have no grape vines.
- Place the uncovered fillets on the foil, directly on the grill, with the grape vines to their side; cover the grill and cook until a knife penetrates the fillet easily.
- Slide a cookie sheet under the foil to carry the fish to the table. Serve by lifting the fillets off the skin with a spatula. Garnish with some lemon slices.

Fred Overton's Clam Chowder
(From his grandmother, Margaret Miller)

- Clean and open clams, grind raw clams in meat grinder, using a coarse blade. Save all juice and strain in cheesecloth.
- Grind raw potatoes to equal the amount of ground clams.
- Grind about two large onions per quart of clams and one 28-oz. can of whole, peeled tomatoes.
- Save the juice. You need one quart of clam juice for each quart of ground clams and an equal amount of tomato juice with water added. Save the liquids.
- Cut 3 or 4 slices of salt pork in 1/2-inch strips. Cook pork in deep pot until browned.
- Add all liquids and onion, tomatoes, and potatoes to the pot.
- Cook until potatoes are very soft. Add clams to boiling soup and stir. When soup returns to a boil, remove from heat immediately and enjoy. A pinch of thyme may be added when you add the clams to the soup. DO NOT boil the clams too long — they will get tough!

Note: Save any clam juice from any prior raw clam feasting to use for clam broth in soup. Freeze until needed.

Above: Fred Overton dishing up his clam chowder at the Trustee's Clam Contest (Photo by Sylvia Mendelman)

Sylvia's Beach Plum/Blueberry Syrup

- Simmer 1 quart very ripe beach plums and 1 quart blueberries in 1 cup water until soft.
- Rub the mixture through a colander. Mix the juice extracted with 1 cup honey, more or less to taste. If the syrup is too thick, add water; if it is too thin, simmer over medium heat until thickened.
- Cool.
- Pour over ice cream, pancakes, grilled chicken, or whatever you choose for a unique, tasty, and healthy treat.

Early Settlers Samp (meatless) or Seaump (with meat), also called Hasty Pudding

Note: The corn was pounded in a hollowed-out tree stump and winnowed to remove the husks.

- Soak together in water overnight:
  - 2 cups cracked corn (samp)
  - 1 cup pea beans or marrow beans
- Drain.
- Simmer in 4 quarts of salted water:
  - samp
  - beans
  - 2 pounds meat (chicken or pork)
- After 3 hours, cool down, and skim off fat.
- Reheat and serve.

Roads and Development

*T*he roads first began to be laid out along Three Mile Harbor in 1701. Town Records indicate that the "highway be laid out beginning at ye head of Three Mile Harbor and continuing on the east side of the harbor to the mouth of said harbor consisting of 4 rods (1 rod = 5.5 yards) in breadth from the fenced land and meadow as it is now fenced; and one highway consisting of 2 rods wide turning out of the above said highway through the land of Robert More down to the harbor to a place called Maskils' landing…. One highway 2 rods wide down to the harbor to the place of going over to the mouth of the harbor."

Three Mile Harbor, L. I.

Above: *Scene of Head of the Harbor, with buggy in foreground (Postcard from the Harvey Ginsberg Collection at East Hampton Library)*
Facing Page: *"Twilight, Three Mile Harbor Road," a copper-plate etching done by Mary Nimmo Moran in 1880 (Courtesy of Guild Hall's Permanent Collection)*

In 1932, George Sid Miller, the Superintendent of Highways, hired people for one dollar a day, scraping and pulling carts to improve the roadbed of "Penny Highway" (currently Three Mile Harbor Road/Hog Creek Highway). Access to the northern end of the Harbor was now easier for cars and trucks.

A fisherman once told me that clam shells made excellent material for a driveway. Thinking to improve my dirt driveway, I had a load dumped and spread them out. The next few weeks were like living next to the Town Dump, because the shells were not dried out yet and reeked of rotten clam. Not only was the driveway stinky, but also my car, because the shells wedged into the tires, and rotten clam followed me wherever I drove. After a few months, fortunately, all was finally back to normal. The shells disappeared into the dirt, the stench was gone, and the driveway was the same as before.

The roads were simple dirt roads — merely cow paths — and wagon wheels formed deep ruts in them. The poor road conditions made it difficult for fishermen to get to their boat landings, launch their boats, and haul their catch to market.

The oldest road to the Springs was Old Accabonac Highway, enabling East Hampton Village access to the East Side's salt marsh hay, seaweed, and cord wood. The Springs was settled in the 1730s, mainly along Springs Fireplace Road. Rumors in 1899 predicted good roads going from Main Street to Three Mile Harbor by 1910. *The East Hampton Star* wrote, "That excellent harbor is now waiting to be developed by the progressive people of this town." Development increased in 1911, and many maps were filed, creating small parcels.

The road from the Head of the Harbor south to the intersection with Fireplace Road was finally paved in the 1930s as a Public Works Administration "Farm to Market Road." Clam and oyster shells, an abundant local resource, were incorporated into the concrete. The shells can still be seen in the road today.

Local investors formed the Harbor Heights Realty Corporation in the 1930s. They purchased the properties of Daniel S. Edwards and Albert Payne, an estimated 65 acres. The property was divided into lots, and Harbor View Avenue gave access down to the water, where some lots on Outlook Avenue were sold for only $150! Dredging was proposed on the northern end of Sedge Island as well as a foot bridge to give people access to a good beach. The initial buyers who built homes there were Smith, Magnus, Waterbury, Ansell, Withers, Dunlop, Johnson, Steele, Fithian, and Talmage.

Peter Bistrian bought property in the Maidstone Park area at a tax sale and named Barry and Bruce Lanes after his sons, and Mary Street after his wife.

Folkstone, located on the northeastern side, was developed in the 1960s by Folke and Chadwick. A boat basin was dredged out of the little cove there for the use of the homeowners. It is privately maintained.

Lion Head development on the west side of Hog Creek is named for a rock shaped like a lion's head, jutting from Gardiners Bay, close to the shore. The Lion Head Property Owners' Association built and continues to maintain a marina in Hog Creek. Dredging the inlet is an expense shared with the Clearwater Beach Property Owners' Association.

The **Clearwater Beach** development is on the eastern side of Hog Creek, extending to Springs Fireplace Road. It was a popular pasture ground before development. Before houses were built in Clearwater, Police Chief Harry Steele (the only policeman in East Hampton in the thirties) shared ownership of a camp/shack/house on the beach with George Sid Miller and Harry Lester. They called it Port of Missing Women or Port of Missing Men, so named because at first the wives would gather to go skinny dipping and soon after the men decided to be "missing" too. It was the only house between Maidstone Park and Fireplace Lodge. There was no running water, and it was heated by a coal stove. Local teenagers eventually started to hang out there, too, building bonfires on the beach and enjoying themselves. Aileen Talmage, Mary Louise Dodge, and John Lester have fond memories of the great parties at the beach there. The shack is still standing, to the west of Lion Head, but it has been renovated and incorporated into a larger house.

Chief Steele had no problem being the only police officer in town. Crime was less common then. People looked after one another and treated each other's possessions with respect. Houses were never locked back in the 1930s, because someone "might have to come in." Neighborliness was the true crimefighter. The good old days!

A map of 1953 shows 150 acres called the **Griffin Farm.** In 1956, Boris Gertzen Associates, Inc., bought 700 acres from Hog Creek to Springs Fireplace Road and named the tract Whispering Woods. Griffin promised to preserve the rustic beauty of the land and to uphold local traditions. Then, Walter Hewitt bought the property and started selling half-acre lots in 1958.

In 1968, the Clearwater Property Owners' Association was formed and a marina basin and beach access was built for its residents. Access by the public to the waters in Hog Creek have been controversial topics and have caused heated debates.

Al Froehlich was the developer of **Settlers Landing and Hampton Waters** in the 1950s on the western shores of Three Mile Harbor. Homes in the Hampton Waters development were built over a dirt trail called Old Indian Highway. Springy Banks Road became the new road, paralleling the Harbor.

Rudy DeSanti, Sr., and his brother-in-law Augie Dragotta developed **Sunnydale Acres,** named after a community in the Dick Tracy comic strip as a joke because everybody laughed at them for buying 150 acres of such "worthless" property. These 150 acres extended from Three Mile Harbor Road to Springs Fireplace Road, along Woodbine Drive (named after Mel Wood, the surveyor).

There is a remnant of a never-finished hotel on the northern corner of Abraham's Path and Three Mile Harbor Road. The stucco building was part of a huge hotel envisioned there, but it was never completed. Its other wooden structures burned down before the hotel could be finished.

Olympic Heights is an area south of the Harbor, where a proposed real estate development in 1913 never developed. The stone pillars marking the entry to this dream gone sour are still there, covered with vines and creating a little bit of nostalgia for old-timers.

Developments were sometimes named so that investors would think that they were buying land in Montauk. Areas around the southern end of Three Mile Harbor Road were called Montauk Lawns, Montauk Manor, Montauk View, and Montauk Estates.

The Stock Market crash and the Great Depression ended many visions of development here until after World War II.

The waters of Three Mile Harbor are split down the middle of the Harbor between two school districts; namely, Springs on the east and East Hampton on the west. Abraham's Path also divides the districts, with Springs being on the north. Springs School offers kindergarten through eighth grade. East Hampton provides the high school on a tuition basis to Springs taxpayers. ❦

OLYMPIC HEIGHTS HOTEL
NEAR THREE MILE HARBOR
EAST HAMPTON LONG ISLAND
E. S. SHAFTER ARCH.
BARNET CONT. CO. BLDRS.

VIEWS OF
OLYMPIC HEIGHTS
& THREE MILE HARBOR
EAST HAMPTON
L. I.

ORNAMENTAL COLUMNS
AT ENTRANCE OLYMPIC HEIGHTS

NEW KENTUCKY BUNGALOW
ERECTED AT OLYMPIC HEIGHTS

LOOKING UP
BAY VIEW AVE
OLYMPIC HEIGHTS

VIEW OF THREE MILE HARBOR FROM
ROADWAY OLYMPIC HEIGHTS EXTENSION

VIEW OF THREE MILE HARBOR 300 FEET
FROM OLYMPIC HEIGHTS EXTENSION

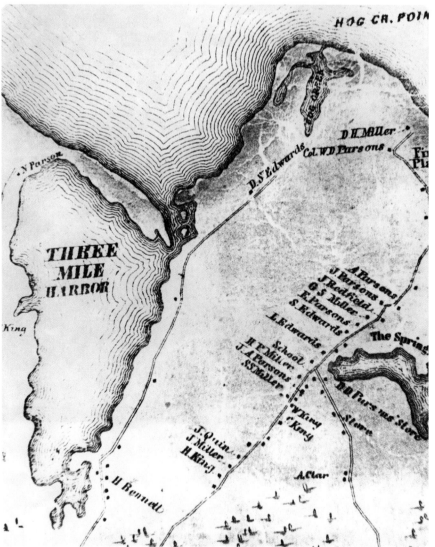

Top: *The Franklin Farmhouse (Photo courtesy of Abigail Edwards Field)*
Left: *Location of the Edwards farm (Franklin Farm) as shown in the 1858 map by Chace (Courtesy of the Amagansett Library)*
Right: *Abigail Edwards Field, at 103, is proudly displaying her fine quilt-making. She celebrated her 105th birthday on April 15, 2003. (Photo by Sylvia Mendelman during an interview)*

The Franklin Farm

The Franklin Farm was an extensive piece of land that extended from Hog Creek and encompassed what is now the Blue Bay Girl Scout Camp, Maidstone Park, and land southward to the Duck Creek Farm near Squaw Road. The farm, originally owned by John and Mary Gardiner, was bought in 1795 by Isaac Edwards, a Revolutionary War soldier. He gave the land to his three sons: Henry went to Barnes Hole, John moved to Duck Creek, and Isaac lived at the end of Hog Creek. A tombstone inscribed "Isaac Edwards" and dated 1823 is on the corner of Flaggy Hole Road and Three Mile Harbor Road.

The farm changed ownership several times. Isaac King was one of the owners until 1881, when John Dudley Edwards bought it back so the farm was once more owned by the family. John's two sons, Samuel and Daniel, shared ownership of it. Samuel Edwards lived on the southern part at Duck Creek. During World War I, this piece was sold to David Gardiner, who eventually sold it in 1951 to John Little, the abstract artist.

Daniel had the northern end of the Franklin Farm, between Maidstone Park and Hog Creek. Abigail Edwards Field, his daughter, and her husband, Herbert Field, ran the farm. A small farmhouse, with two and a half stories, was enlarged with the addition of another house belonging to Seth Parsons. There were two chimneys ten feet square in the middle of the house. When Abigail's grandfather, John Dudley Edwards, took down the dividing walls, his wife exclaimed, "Now the kitchen is so big you can sling a cat in it!"

The farm was known for its wheat, the hardest and best in East Hampton. Charles Dominy, the miller, had the highest praise for it. There were between 50 to 60 acres under cultivation.

Abigail fondly remembers a percheron horse they acquired named Prince. The horse had been part of a paired carriage team, but since the owner wanted horses with matching colors, he sold Prince to the Fields. He was very much loved by the family.

Abigail recalls that during the Depression, her husband, Herbert, was too proud to buy "welfare clothes." If people commented on the darned holes in his clothes, he replied, "Don't you like my embroidery?"

Almost everyone during the Depression had to have two trades to survive. Abigail's husband was a farmer and a fisherman. Her brother Sam owned a 38-foot boat named *Gertrude*, which capsized during the hurricane of 1938 while he was trap fishing. The crew had wanted to finish fixing the nets before the storm hit, thinking it just another Nor'easter, but the 20-foot surge and fierce winds were no match for them. Abigail's husband, Herb, her two brothers, Gilbert and Sam, and Vivian Smith all perished. Sam's body was washed ashore at Block Island, but the others were never found. Abigail was left a widow with four children. She couldn't run the farm alone, so the family moved to the Village. As Abigail said, "It bothered my time of day" to live through the effects of the Depression, being a widow and having four children to support!

A portion of the original 200-year-old house from the Franklin Farm was moved to the triangle by Skimhampton Road and Montauk Highway. This area is known as Franklin Triangle in East Hampton.

Abigail was born on April 15, 1898, and participated in the festivities for East Hampton's 350th anniversary of its founding on October 10, 1998. She was 100 years old at the time of the parade! 🦪

Hurricanes

The sheltered location of Three Mile Harbor usually prevents major storm damage to boats and houses, but there have been some storms in which the wind direction coupled with a surging tide have caused severe devastation to boats, houses, and the shoreline.

Facing Page: An awesome bolt of lightning over the Harbor (Photo © 2001 by Gordon M. Grant)
Above Left: *Wreck of the* Angler, *beached by the 1938 hurricane; owner was Mr. Vail, father of Emerson Taber (Photo courtesy of the East Hampton Historical Society)*
Above Right: *Boats washed ashore in Three Mile Harbor after Hurricane Bob, August 19, 1991 (Photo © 2001 by Gordon M. Grant)*

The hurricane of 1938 did much damage to the houses, trees, and small boats on and along Three Mile Harbor. Many were swept up on the beach, and some boats were swept out to sea through the mouth of the Harbor. Docks, bulkheads, and homes were damaged by flooding. Thankfully, Wessberg's Boat Yard, Palmer's Docks, and Halsey's Marina had little damage.

The *Leila T.*, a boat owned by John Howard, was blown onto the beach, as was the *Kema*, owned by Mayor Judson Bannister. The only boat blown ashore at the Head of the Harbor was the *Cairn Hill,* owned by Phillip Ruxton. There was no warning of this storm's force, and it caused widespread devastation.

Isabel Gardiner Mairs remembers being on a 400-foot yacht that night, just outside the Harbor. On board were Howard Hughes, Hoagy Carmichael, and many socialites intent on going to Bermuda for an excursion. The weather forced the captain to cancel the voyage, but to make it back to shore, they had to take a series of small launches through the jetty of Three Mile Harbor. The waves and wind made the trip to shore treacherous, but fortunately they all made it back safely.

Other storms are well remembered also, such as the 1917 Nor'easter that flooded the roads, submerging the bridge by Pussy's Pond, and the 90-mile-an-hour gale on August 26, 1924, which sank quite a few boats. In 1954, Hurricane Carol had winds of 130 miles an hour.

Ice storms and winds very often take down electric poles, causing lengthy outages. I remember outages from hurricanes Gloria (September 27, 1985) and Bob (August 19, 1991). Luckily, the Harbor's waters were still warm, so we would have a dip in the water to wash up since we couldn't pump water from the well. We used grills to cook our food and brought home buckets of water for flushing toilets. Candlelight was necessary when the flashlights burned out. We just kept farmer's hours and went to bed when it got dark. The Fire Department helped pump out basements, and the community pulled together. Springs School allowed the public use of their showers and facilities. The community still takes hurricanes very seriously and prepares for the worst. People help each other out if disaster strikes. Neighborliness is just a matter of fact here in East Hampton. 🐚

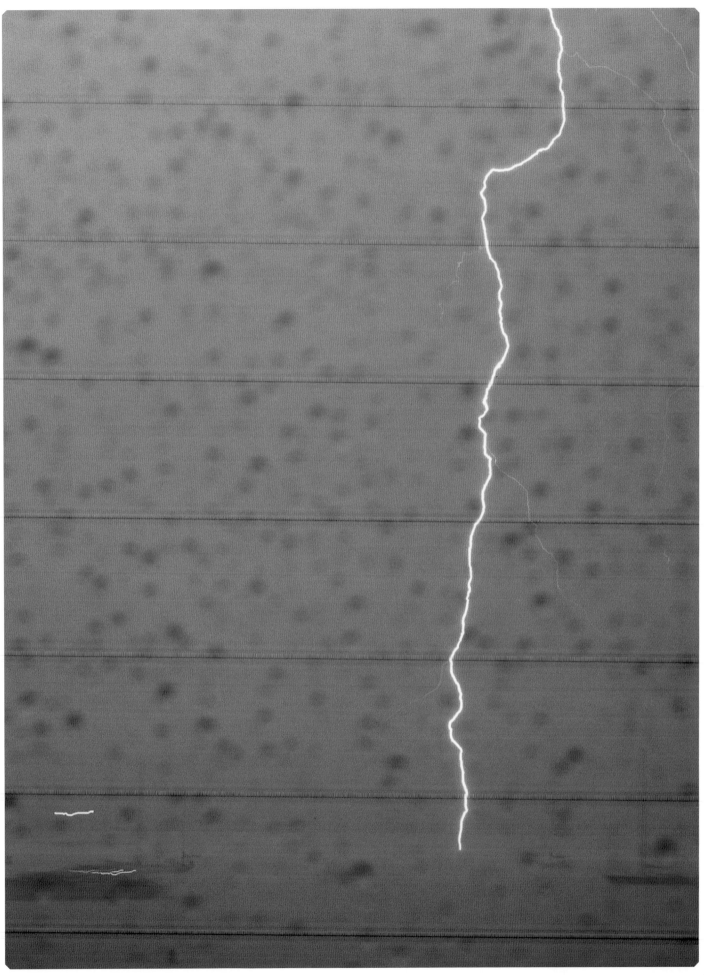

The Art Colony

Ask any artist why East Hampton is so special and the answer is, "the light!" The "island light" is especially unique to this area. When skies are clear, the visibility can be more than 14 miles. The dazzle of the midday summer sun contrasts with the soft rosy glow of dawn. Early morning mists hover over the water until dissipated by the sun's warmth. At day's end, the blinding, intense rays of the sun descending in the horizon are just a prelude to a symphony of color. Clouds become palettes for a mélange of yellow, orange, crimson, and purple. This show is reflected in the water, bringing the masterpiece to our level—to touch, if you will. The landscape framing the periphery of the Harbor has singular beauty in the high bluffs, the sandy and rocky shoreline, the beach grasses, and the verdant forests. If an artist needed more subject matter, there is also the variety of marine life, birds, animals, boats, and people.

East Hampton started to become well known when William Cullen Bryant published *Picturesque America* in 1876, in which an article acclaimed, "perhaps no town in America retains so nearly the primitive habits, tastes, and ideas of our forefathers as East Hampton." East Hampton offered artists a rural lifestyle with aesthetics and affordability.

The Harbor has attracted many well-known artists to East Hampton, among them Winslow Homer, Thomas Moran, Mary Nimmo Moran, Edward Moran, Walter Granville Smith, Mauritz DeHaas, Arthur Quartley (founder of the Tile Club), and others.

The famous Tile Club, organized by Arthur Quartley from 1877 to 1890, was a semi-social artists and writers society. They created art tiles in New York City and also when they gathered in East Hampton. Their club was nicknamed "Marine" because Quartley liked maritime subjects and his emblem was a ship.

By 1885, *Century Magazine* described East Hampton as a "true artist colony," with "beach and sea panoramas, stormy cloud-battles, or shimmering calm for the marine-painter… here are salt sea-breezes and sunshine for all." Painting done *en plein air* was the vogue, and outdoor scenes were very popular.

The number of scenes of East Hampton exhibited by artists in New York City tripled between 1880 and 1890. City dwellers were attracted to East Hampton because of these scenes, and the tourist industry became the biggest industry in East Hampton Village by 1890. Childe Hassam (Horseham) visited East Hampton in 1898. After coming here for several summers, he finally bought a house in 1919.

The earliest artists' group society show was held at the Clinton Academy in 1929. Childe Hassam said, "My ancestors were just like yours — New England farmers and sailors." In 1923, he had warned, "East Hampton could very easily be made into a combed and manicured suburb — a New Rochelle — but it must not happen." His words still ring true.

Some other artists who came here in the 1930s were Francis and Richard Newton, Hamilton King, William J. Whittemore, and Albert Herter.

The 1940 and 1950s were the years that the avant-garde abstract artists gathered in East Hampton. Jackson Pollock moved here with Lee Krasner in 1945 and bought a home on Springs-Fireplace Road with a loan from Peggy Guggenheim, his patron and dealer. His retort when asked why he didn't paint nature was, "I am nature."

Painter En Plein Air at Pussy's Pond (Watercolor by Scott Hewett)

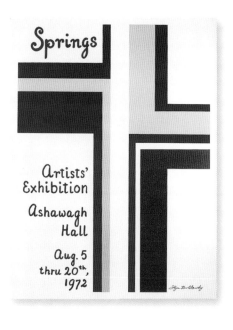

Springs
Artists'
Exhibition
Ashawagh
Hall
Aug. 5
thru 20th,
1972

the Springs
Artists' Exhibition
August 4 thru the 19th, 1973
Ashawagh Hall

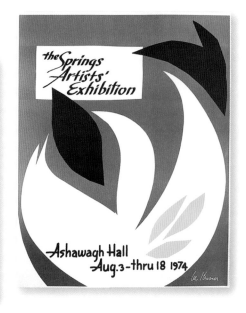

the Springs
Artists'
Exhibition
Ashawagh Hall
Aug. 3 - thru 18 1974

springs artists exhibition
ashawagh hall · august 4-19 1979

ashawagh hall springs artists exhibition
august 2-17 1980

springs
artists
exhibition

ASHAWAGH
HALL
SAT. AUG. 1
THRU
SUN. AUG. 16

THE SPR

ASHAWAG

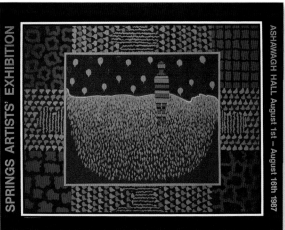

SPRINGS ARTISTS' EXHIBITION

ASHAWAGH HALL August 1st — August 16th 1987

SPRINGS ARTISTS' EXHIBITION

ASHAWAGH HALL August 6th — August 20th 1988

SPRINGS ARTISTS EXHIBITION
Ashawagh Hall

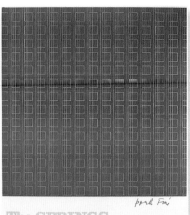

The SPRINGS
ARTISTS EXHIBITION
ASHAWAGH HALL Aug 7 thru Aug 21

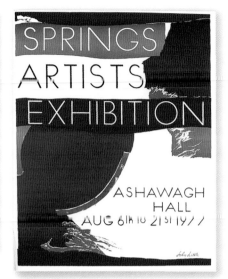

SPRINGS
ARTISTS
EXHIBITION

ASHAWAGH
HALL
AUG 6th to 21st 1977

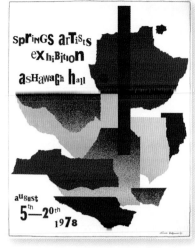

spRinGS arTisTs
eXhiBiTion
asHawaGh hall

august
5th—20th
1978

...TS EXHIBITION

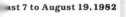

...st 7 to August 19, 1982

SPRINGS ARTISTS EXHIBITION
ASHAWAGH HALL

August 6
to 20
1983

the Springs
Artists'
Exhibition

Ashawagh Hall
Aug. 3 thru 18 1985

EXHIBITION

SPRINGS
ARTISTS — AUG. 2-17
ASHAWAGH HALL

springs ▪ artists ▪ exhibition   AUG. 4 THRU AUG. 18
ASHAWAGH HALL

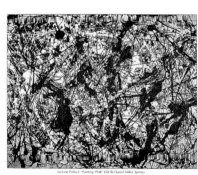

Jackson Pollock "Painting 1948" Gift to Daniel Miller, Springs

THIRTIETH ANNUAL
SPRINGS ARTISTS EXHIBITION
ASHAWAGH HALL   AUGUST 1 - 17, 1997

© 1997 POLLOCK - KRASNER FOUNDATION / ARS NY

77

Abstract artist John Little and his wife, Josephine, settled on Three Mile Harbor after a visit with Jackson Pollock and Lee Krasner in 1948. They purchased farmland owned by J. T. Gardiner at Duck Creek Farm, fixed up a hundred-year-old roofless house, and started to raise their family. A barn from the Gardiner property on James Lane in the village was moved up to their property and became the studio for John Little. They enjoyed their beautiful property, relished the "Gardiner's peaches" that grew on their trees, and shared the beauty of the sunsets and the boat regattas in Three Mile Harbor with their friends.

Willem deKooning, another abstract expressionist, settled on land off Woodbine Drive in 1963, between Three Mile Harbor Road and Springs Fireplace Road. His work captured the mellow, muted colors of the sand and sunshine reflected in the water. He was fascinated with the light's tendency to change form when interacting with water.

The Pavias also came out to settle here. In 1977, they moved a potato barn from Southold to Squaw Road by floating it over the bay to the Commercial Dock near Gann Road. It became their house and studio. Philip Pavia was the first abstract expressionist in stone sculpture. His wife, Natalie Edgar, is a painter. Their son Paul sculpts in metal.

Other artists drawn to the area because of its beauty and affordability at that time included David Porter, Ron Marcarelli, Wilfrid Zogbaum, Jim Brooks, Perle Fine, Alfonso Ossorio, Linda Lindberg, Robert Motherwell, Franz Kline, Nicholas Carone, Charlotte Park, Ibram Lassaw, and Ray Parker, among many others.

Ralph Carpentier, whose love of the water is reflected in his paintings, is currently a local artist who lives in Springs. He is the former director of the East Hampton Town Marine Museum in Amagansett and has assisted them with nautical displays and painted murals depicting scenes of fishing and whaling.

Contemporary painters, sculptors, potters, and photographers — such as Lauren Jarrett, Randy Rosenthal, Nicole Bigar, Norman Mercer, John Alexander, Scott Hewett, Randy Handwerger, Ken Robbins, Doug Kuntz, Gordon Grant, Morgan McGivern, and many, many more — have all been inspired by this area.

The Springs Art Show is now an annual event at Ashawagh Hall in August. This is an invitational show that exhibits a large variety of works by local artists. Guild Hall in the Village has a permanent collection of some of these artists. 🍂

Summer Camps

The eastern shore of Three Mile Harbor was built up with many small summer houses in the 1900s. East Hampton Village had very few hotels for summer vacationers, resulting in a lack of accommodations. Seizing the opportunities, many townspeople rented out their homes in the Village and left for the shores of Three Mile Harbor to "camp" for the summer. Some villagers didn't want to rent their homes in the village, but they brought their families to their camps at the Harbor anyway in order to enjoy the summer there. These "campers" became a close-knit community, and many strong friendships developed.

VIEW OF THREE MILE HARBOR, EAST HAMPTON, L.I.   100437

Head of the Harbor with view of camps along eastern shore (Postcard from the Harvey Ginsberg Collection at East Hampton Library)

Some of the cottages on the eastern shore, going north from the Head of the Harbor belonged to Bill Bain, Edward Tillinghast, James Reilly, Andrew Carson, Gardiner Osborne, Ed Osborne, Nelson Osborne, John Meeker, Jay Mulford, Nathan Dayton, Grandma Hatch, Richard Herrlin, Dr. John Herrlin, Harry Jeffreys, Ernest Miller (sold to Robert Lynch), George Eldridge, Mr. Vail (sold to Darrell Parsons, who sold to Ronald Rioux), Newt and Helen Tiffany, Robert Proctor, Max and Carl Reutershan (sold to Percy Schenck), and Judson Bannister. North of Shagwong was Juan Trippe's seaplane hanger and the homes of Olly Miller, Budd and Beryl King, and Willard Livingston (sold to Michael Helm). Many of these cottages have since been winterized and have become homes for "year-rounders."

Carrie Tillinghast said that their house on Will Curl Highway was moved to Three Mile Harbor from Stony Hill in 1946. Carrie remembered the cold February of 1934 when she and her husband, Ed, joined by Budd and Beryl King and the Tiffanys, walked over the ice to Gardiner's Island to have lunch with the caretaker, Jock Mackay. They walked the five miles back, too! 🍂

Boys Harbor

*T*his campsite for young people was started in 1954 by Anthony Drexel Duke on the western shores of Three Mile Harbor. The 26-acre parcel of land south of Hands Creek has given girls and boys from New York City the opportunity to experience the country. Tony Duke and his wife, Luly, believe in empowering the lives of inner-city young people, helping them overcome adversity as they achieve their creative, intellectual, and economic dreams. Boys Harbor was formerly under the direction of Lonnie Williams, who passed away recently. A rock greets campers to the facility, which came to be named Lonnie's Rock, since it was his favorite place to sit and talk to troubled campers. The programs have expanded their sphere to encompass a year-round facility on 104th Street and Fifth Avenue in New York City, for preschoolers through high school students. The Dukes continue to help youths at every economic and social level to be properly educated, giving them opportunities for their futures and, ultimately, for the improvement of our society.

Above: Boys Harbor Logo (Designed by Diane C. Hewett, 2000)
Right: Tony Duke leading his campers up the dock (Photo courtesy of Anthony D. Duke)
Facing Page: Boys Harbor Fireworks, an annual fund-raiser is hosted by the Dukes, with commentary by George Plimpton. Hundreds of boats fill the Harbor every year to view one of the best fireworks displays in town. (Photo ©2001 by Gordon M. Grant)

Boys Harbor holds an annual fund-raiser in mid-July. There is a late-afternoon picnic on the grounds, followed by fireworks at dusk. George Plimpton has narrated the displays, giving colorful descriptions and honorary tributes for each burst that goes off. Three Mile Harbor fills with boats from all over the Northeast, and the shores crowd with people eager to enjoy the spectacular display.

The local schools have also used the facility to enrich their curriculum. The Harbor Environmental Research Center was started in 1997 to increase the awareness of children to outdoor exploration and appreciation of our natural resources. The program was a highly successful adjunct to the curriculum in the schools. The name of the camp has recently been changed to Boys and Girls Harbor.

6169   THREE MILE HARBOR, L. I.   PUBL, BY W. J. HOPPER, EAST HAMPTON, L. I.

Marinas in the Harbor

n the 1900s, the arrival of larger boats and the expansion of the shellfish industry stimulated the need for proper facilities for docking the boats and unloading the catch. In 1901, J. T. Gardiner applied to the Trustees for a "landing stage" at the Head of Three Mile Harbor for the accommodation of the public.

A committee headed by J. T. Gardiner and C. G. Thompson of the Maidstone Club was largely influential in securing the necessary dredging and breakwater for Three Mile Harbor.

John Hand circulated a petition in 1904 for the improvement of Three Mile Harbor with a dock at Springy Banks. He said that East Hampton's Harbor would become a busy place for the boatmen and the financial benefit to this town would be beyond all expectations. That same year, a bill was presented to the Secretary of War to survey and submit plans and estimates for the dredging of a channel.

The leisure boats of the wealthy were soon coming into the Harbor. A 47-foot sloop, the *Ilderan*, owned by Grimshaw and Culver, sailed into the Harbor in 1906, joined by A. B. Terry's boat *Cleo* and, in 1907, by L. E. Woodhouse's launch.

J. T. Gardiner was given permission to extend his marine railways in 1906. By 1908, with still no improvement to the Harbor, the Harbor's shellfish industry giants — J. T. Gardiner, David J. Gardiner, and Samuel Grimshaw — took matters into their own hands. They secured $10,000 from a private loan, and through the efforts of John Hand and Assemblyman DeWitt Talmage, obtained another $10,000 in federal and state aid. They built two stone breakwaters at the mouth of the Harbor with stone from Connecticut and did the dredging necessary for the navigation of boats.

The Maidstone Boat Club was formed in 1914, with J. T. Gardiner, Tyson Dominy, and Jeremiah Huntting as its founders and governing committee. They raised $1,350 and installed channel markers to Gardiner's Bay.

The Trustees authorized the club to cut through Long Beach shoal, creating a channel on its eastern end. They also allowed them to bulkhead and dredge in front of their property at the Head of the Harbor. This bulkhead was approved in 1916 for Culver, Gardiner, McAlpin, and the Maidstone Boat Club. Ralph Preston built the Maidstone Club's bulkhead in 1916.

Frank B. Wiborg also encouraged improvements to Three Mile Harbor in the 1920s. Navigational safety was such a concern in 1926 that Paul Wiborg succeeded in having the department of the Secretary of the War send engineers to make an inspection of Three Mile Harbor. In 1930, the Town Board voted to spend $11,000 to improve the breakwater. By 1931, the channel was dredged to more than 10 feet in depth and 100 feet in length. The Town of East Hampton approved $55,000 for new jetties, dredging, and a public dock. Boats with 12-foot drafts could now dock easily. Henry R. Sutphen, head of the National Association of Engine and Boat Manufacturers, whose Electric Boat Company built submarine chasers and pleasure boats, kept his cruiser in the Harbor.

The Town Board recognized the need for regulations in the Harbor, and in 1932 they ruled that there could be no mooring within 100 feet of the bulkhead and declared it unlawful to dump into the waters of Three Mile Harbor.

A light at the entrance to the Harbor was installed in 1932 by the Maidstone Boat Club, and Captain Hussey was hired to maintain it.

Facing Page, Top: *Three Mile Harbor (Postcard courtesy of East Hampton Library)*
Facing Page, Bottom: *Postcard with view looking toward the Town Dock in the 1950s (Photo © by Milt Price)*

Navigation was still considered dangerous in 1933.
When the motor ship *Solarina* of Philadelphia
arrived at 4 A.M. carrying 5,216 bags of fertilizer
from Maryland, Captain Earl Carlisle commented,
"What a nice little harbor, but there are no lights,
and it is very dangerous to navigation."

Ludlow Raynor was hired to take care of the channel markers. They were made of green oak, with
port and starboard indicators on top. Kerosene
lamps were mounted on them, and they had to
be filled regularly.

The Maidstone Boat Club's docks eventually
became the property of the Town of East Hampton.
The Trustees proposed an amendment in 1941
to the ordinance regarding the Town Dock at
the Head of the Harbor. It read, "The entire dock
be open to the public for the taking on and dis-
charging of passengers or merchandise and that
no one boat be allowed to remain at the dock for
a period longer than four hours during any one
calendar day from May 15th until September 15th
inclusive of each and every year; also, the outer
end of the dock be open at all times."

Today, the Town of East Hampton leases slips at
this dock on a seasonal basis to residents at far
below the going rate. The cost of the dock, electricity, and slips is subsidized by the East Hampton
Town taxpayers. A slip space is assured to the boat
owner until the boat owner either does not pay the
annual fee or decides not to keep the slip. Naturally,
the Town has a long waiting list for these slips.

Buoys were stationed permanently in their places
in the channel and entered on the U.S. Coast and
Geodetic Survey in 1962. They were painted and
numbered according to U.S. Coast Guard regulations. The tops had reflective tape, so they would
pick up light at night. Bruce Collins, the chairman
of the Town Board's Harbors and Docks Committee,
handled this project, which was well received by
the boaters. A steel jetty on the west side of the
inlet was installed. In 1965, this steel jetty was
replaced with a stone groin at a cost of $150,000.

Dredging of the channel in the Harbor was done
by Suffolk County in 1938, 1950, 1976, and 1999.
The huge amount of dredged material that had
accumulated between 1976 and 1999 was depos-

ited in a catch basin dug out in Sammy's Beach. The catch basin was so big it defaced the nature preserve. When the residents near Sammy's Beach protested, East Hampton Town tried to restore the vegetation there.

The Head of the Harbor had the first boatyard in Three Mile Harbor, which was owned by Joe Miller. In 1930, it was bought by Harry Wessberg. Boats had to be hauled out on rails by hand or by horse. The boats were left to dry, painted, and pushed back in the water. In 1935, Wessberg asked for a permit from the Trustees to build a dock. He paid the fixed $15 annual dock permit fee and improved the facility.

Bob Story bought Wessberg's **Three Mile Harbor Boatyard** in 1950, and his son, Sam, is the current owner. Improvements were made in 1953. A new bulkhead, L-shaped pier, and mooring piles were installed. The old system for hauling boats was replaced with a Marine Travelift, and the facility also added a marine store.

Heading west on Boatyard Road are two more marinas, East Hampton Marina and Three Mile Marina. **East Hampton Marina** was first developed in 1950 by Leon Raucher. In 1972, Geoffrey Briggs bought it, installed bulk-heading, put in docks for 65 slips, and bought a forklift to haul boats. The marina also has a repair shop and parts store, specializing in Mercury outboards.

Adjacent to East Hampton Marina is **Three Mile Marina,** which was developed by Donald Vanderveer in 1957. In 1968, he installed floats and pilings extending out from the shoreline. Small boats are docked there and hauled with a crane/straps rig.

Right: Gardiner's Marina, summer 2000 (Photo by Diane C. Hewett)
Middle: Oscar Mott's shack on the shores of the Harbor, removed when Gardiner's Marina was developed (Photo courtesy of Patricia Field)
Bottom: Robert L.D. Gardiner docking at his newly built marina in his boat Laughing Lady, *first owned by Mrs. Bradley, who lived in the Cedar Point Lighthouse (Photo courtesy of Patricia Field)*

Proceeding north along the eastern shore from the Town Dock at the Head of the Harbor is **Gardiner's Marina.** Robert David Lion Gardiner developed this boat basin during the 1950s. Oscar Mott had a boathouse there before Gardiner bought it. Another house just north of the marina was moved to Isabel Gardiner Mairs' property on James Lane in the village. The boat basin was dredged and land filled in to create Gardiner's Marina, with 45 slips. It was sold in 1999 to the Mendelman sons, Peter and Mark, who hope to maintain the historic character of this sheltered cove. A Gardiner's family crest can be seen on the sign at the entrance to the marina.

Halsey's Marina was established in 1923. The Maidstone Boat Club had its headquarters there in the summertime and used the village offices at the Osborne Insurance Agency in the winter. In 1931, I.Y. Halsey bought the waterfront property from Leander (Lam) Bennett. Lam was allowed the rights to use the freshwater well on the property. Stones marking the well are still there today. Halsey applied for a permit to build a T-shaped dock for his marina in 1949, but it was rejected by the Trustees because it was too wide. He eventually received permission for docks and installed 40 slips.

In 1959, the Three Mile Harbor Yacht Club was headquartered at Halsey's Marina, with Edward Monroe Osborne as its Commodore. Members included Ed Tillinghast, Nelson Osborne, Jr., David Collins, James Reilly, and Charles White Hand. The property was sold in the 1980s to an investment group. Stanley Becker, one of the group, remembered a year that flooding from a hurricane was so high that it filled the clothes dryers in the clubhouse.

In 1993, the marina hosted a "Camper-Nicholson" regatta, with 25 boats participating in the weekend festivities. Peter Mendelman is currently the new owner and lives on the property with his family.

Shagwong Marina is located on a former swamp known as the Black Meadow or Black Marsh.

Juan Trippe, the founder of Pan-American Airlines, built a seaplane hanger in the late thirties on the shore at this site and would land his Aeromarine single-pontoon seaplane here. He had another seaplane landing base in Georgica Pond. Having summered in East Hampton when he was a child, he enjoyed coming back to visit. He had been an ensign in naval aviation during World War I and became president of the Maidstone Club in 1940.

The Trippe property was eventually bought by the Grom brothers, Emil and Henry. In 1952, they applied for permission to build a boat basin there. Permission was granted by the Trustees and the Town Board in 1954. The Groms dredged out the swamp and bulkheaded the basin. The property was sold to John A. Kappel in 1964, and he and his wife, Katie, built a home on the water's edge. He enlarged the marina from 30 to 40 slips. John and Katie also built and managed summer cottages there, renting them out for the season. After John's death, the marina was sold to Frank Dragotta and Robert Grau in 1986. It was recently renamed Shagwong Marina, the Quiet Cove.

Maidstone Boatyard was started by Stephen A. Palmer because he enjoyed boating and needed to keep his boat somewhere. His daughter Helen fondly remembers sailing with her father and sister Jean on the *Rough Rider*, a Friendship sloop. In the 1930s, wanting to haul his own 28-foot boat the *Valiant*, he rigged up a winch-type system. Soon, he began hauling other boats, too. He requested marine railways and a dock in 1932 from the Trustees and installed an L-shaped dock. In 1936, Palmer dredged out Duck Creek and bulkheaded it. Many people remember that there was once an icehouse on this site.

A restaurant was built there in 1946 called the Silver Seahorse. The dock facility is currently called the **Maidstone Harbor Marina,** and it has slips for 125 boats.

Left, Top: Maidstone Boatyard early 1930s with Duck Creek to its left (Aerial photo by Dave Edwardes; courtesy of Doug Kuntz)
Left, Bottom: Stephen Palmer with daughter Jean, sailing in the Harbor, with Maidstone Boatyard in the background (Photo courtesy of Helen Palmer Edwards)
Above: Duck Creek developed into Maidstone Marina, with East Hampton Point Boatyard and Restaurant in background (Photo courtesy of Walter Cook and Doug Dinizzio)

MAIDSTONE
MARINA

Another restaurant was built south of the Maidstone Boatyard in the 1980's. Cottages were added to the facility by moving old buildings to the site. Among them was the old St. Matthew Church building (a chapel of St. Luke's), originally located southwest of the Neighborhood House on Three Mile Harbor Road. The boatyard/restaurant facility was sold several times over the years. The current owners renamed it **East Hampton Point Restaurant, Cottages, Marina, and Boatyard.**

The **Commercial Dock** at the foot of Gann Road was developed in the 1920s. The property was bought from Jennie T. Edwards by Winthrop Gardiner and Carl Fisher who hoped to have a seaplane landing base and fuel depot there. Interest in aviation was high in the early days of flight, and many people flew back and forth from New York to East Hampton. Clark Gable was a frequent visitor, landing by seaplane in Three Mile Harbor, to the delight of the local girls. Garrett Livingston also landed his seaplane in the Harbor.

In July 1931, the property was cleared of trees, bulkheaded, and graded. Work was completed in July 1934. Gardiner moved a barn from his farm at Duck Creek to the dock for the use of the fishermen as a storage-packing house.

Unfortunately, Gardiner and Fisher felt the effects of the Stock Market crash, and due to lack of funds, the Bank of New York foreclosed on the property. It was ultimately sold to the Town of East Hampton in 1943 for $600. The Town invested $20,000 to repair the bulkhead, realizing the dock's future value to residents. In 1956, it was rezoned for the use of commercial fishermen. The fishermen were permitted to unpack their catch and prepare it for shipment right on the dock. Nets and lobster pots could be dried and stored there, making life for the fishermen a little easier.

Isabel Gardiner Mairs remembered the night she and her girlfriend took their car to the Commercial Dock during Prohibition, because they were curious about what was going on. In the dark of night, they saw some men unloading boxes from a boat and heard a guttural shout, "Babes, go home!" That must have left an impression on her, because she still remembered it during an interview when she was ninety years old!

The building on the Commercial Dock was rented from the Town by Emerson Taber and made into a lobster house with holding tanks, with a cookhouse on the side added later. The dock was called Taber's Dock for a long time. He later sold the business to John Howard and his wife, Pearl, and the name was changed to Howard's Seafood. In the early 1970s, Lee and Mickey Dion carried on the business for a few years, selling fresh lobsters, clams, and homemade clam pies. In the late seventies,

East Hampton Town stopped leasing the land for retail fish market usage and converted the building into The Boat Shop to teach boat-building to the public. After The Boat Shop closed, the Town then used the building as its Harbor Master's headquarters and installed a pump-out station on the southern side of the dock. The original building was moved to Olney (Bill) Gardiner's property on James Lane in the village, and a new building was constructed on the dock in 1999.

The dock still has commercial fishermen tying up to the bulkhead, unpacking their catch, and storing lobster pots, nets, and gear next to their boats. The dock is also a proverbial "backyard fence" for Bonackers. Bub's pickups park side by side, windows are rolled down, and Bonac wisdom, jokes, and the news of the day float in and out of the windows.

Facing Page: Sketch of Jim Taylor's marina with the Commercial Dock and Dayton's Island in background (Artist unknown)
Above: Emerson Taber taking lobster from a pot (Photo courtesy of the East Hampton Historical Society)
Below: Taber's Lobsters at the Commercial Dock, now the site of the Harbor Master's offices; Taber's Lobster House, formerly a barn from Winthrop Gardiner's Duck Creek property, was moved to the Commercial Dock in the 1930s (Photo courtesy of C. E. King)

North of the Commercial Dock at the foot of Gann Road is the **Harbor Marina of East Hampton.** Penny Sedge Island buffers the marina from the channel, affording sheltered dockage. Terns, ospreys, cormorants, sea gulls and other seaside birds make their habitat on the island and on the western side of the channel at Sammy's Beach, town parkland.

Joshua Penny, the War of 1812 hero, lived at the foot of Gann Road next to his brother-in-law John Gann. In 1823, he received permission from the Town to build a wharf in front of his house and lived there until his death in 1840. Captain J. F. Hussey came to live there in 1891 with his wife, Anna V. Chapman, and her half brothers.

In 1931, Captain Hussey asked the Trustees for permission to have a channel dug in the narrow creek between his home and the meadow (Penny Sedge Island), as far north as Harold Dunlop's north line. The channel would make it easier for boats to be moored there and improve his access to the mouth of the Harbor. After Hussey's wife died, he moved to Amagansett in 1948 to be near his wife's brother. The property was sold to James Taylor, who developed a dock 50 feet long in 1950. He had the permits to install the docks, but every night his work on the bulkheading would be destroyed by some locals who were against the idea of the bulkhead. Being a tough retired mounted policeman, he took matters in his own hands. He sat up all night by his bulkhead, gun in hand. Word got

Facing Page: "Drying Nets" on the Commercial Dock (1940s watercolor by Carl Kinscherf)
Above: Aerial view of the Harbor the morning after the fireworks at Boys Harbor (Aerial photo by Eagle Eye Aerial Photography, 1980s)
Left: This sign of Captain Hussey's was found at the Harbor Marina.

CATCH THE BIG ONES
WITH
HUSSEY'S
BOATS AND BAIT

Facing Clockwise From Top: Boats at the Harbor Marina silhouetted by one of many magnificent sunsets that can also be enjoyed from Bostwick's restaurant. (Photo by Diane C. Hewett) • Boat in Marine Travelift ready for launch at the Harbor Marina (Photo by Edna Renner) • Jim Taylor's sign advertising his business was found on the Harbor Marina property. • Cox's Fishing Station, formerly Charlie Weiss's, before its destruction in 1999, on the south side of Maidstone Park (Photo by Randy Handwerger)

around, and he was left alone after that. A relation of his, Carl Petrat, built a house at the foot of Gann Road and also kept his boat along the bulkhead.

Taylor built himself a small, sturdy home on the crest of the hill overlooking the marina. He moved some houses off the property, among them Captain Hussey's house, which was moved up to Three Mile Harbor Road, where it is now the home of Joseph and Mary Fitzgerald. Another old building was moved to the Maidstone Park area so that Jim's brother-in-law Charlie Weiss could operate a fishing station there. **Weiss's Fishing Station** was run as a bait, tackle, and small-boat rental business until it was sold to William and Bunny Cox in 1975. The Coxes added the upper floor, rented small boats, and sold bait, tackle, and frozen Milky Ways (people bait). They ran a very successful business called **Cox's Fishing Station** until Bill's death. The property was sold in 1981 and is currently owned by the Town of East Hampton, which destroyed the old building and bulkhead in 1999 and is letting the property revert to its natural state.

Jim Taylor sold his marina facility of 8.7 acres to investors in 1964 who named it the Harbor Marina of East Hampton, Inc. In 1970, Dick Mendelman arrived to operate the facility and lived in the house on the hill with his wife, Sylvia, and their four children, Lynn, Peter, Diane, and Mark. In 1975, Buck Burnett (Leland J. Burnett, Jr.) shared ownership until the Mendelman family became sole owners

in 1995. The Harbor Marina has slips for 90 boats, a fuel dock, marine store, a boatyard for servicing motors and hull repairs, and year-round storage facilities. There is also a restaurant on the property currently called Bostwick's.

Mansir Marine, owned and operated by Walter Mansir, has been at the Harbor Marina since 1978. His sons also share in the business with trailering, launching, and outboard repairs.

Tucked into the eastern end of the Maidstone Beach peninsula is **Sunset Cove**, a small marina with about 35 slips. Its channel entry is shared with **Folkstone's** basin. Originally developed by Robert Terrison, it is now owned by Mr. and Mrs. George Nicholas.

Currently, there are also 80 public moorings in the Harbor assigned by the Town Trustees on an annual basis. They are located in several designated areas, but the major concentration of moorings is in the southern half of the Harbor. A boater must apply annually for a mooring. There are just six transient moorings available, and boaters must contact the Harbor Master for availability.

Lee's Three Mile Harbor Pavilion
Three Mile Harbor, L. I.

The Lighthouse at Maidstone Village

Elegant Dining on the Waterfront
Brunches Sat. and Sun. 11:30 to 2:00
Luncheon from 11:30 and
Dinner from 5:30
Late Supper 11:00 to 2:00 a.m.
295 Three Mile Harbor Road, East Hampton

Restaurants

A memorable day: September 4, 1886! At exactly three o'clock, a procession of stages wound its way from Ocean Avenue to Three Mile Harbor, picking up people along the way, with much singing and joviality as they traveled to their destination. Arriving at the Harbor, everybody pitched in to prepare a feast of clams, fresh ears of corn, potatoes, and baskets of other treats. Sailboats and rowboats took the parties for rides to explore the coves and shores of the Harbor. At five-thirty, they returned for the long-awaited feast. After a delicious supper and a speech by one who was highly esteemed, everyone got back into their stages and returned home before dark. Such was the annual custom for many years! There were no restaurants along the shores then, but times have changed that.

Restaurants are now very popular along Three Mile Harbor. The water views, fresh fish and shellfish, sunsets, and balmy westerly breezes are a winning combination.

The first restaurant along the Harbor was **Lee's Three Mile Harbor Pavilion.** This popular restaurant, dance hall, and boat rental establishment was built in 1903 by Ulysses Lee and Austin H. Culver. It was located at the Head of the Harbor on the eastern shore, where Karlsruhe Lane is today. Many summer residents gave parties there, among them, Mrs. Gayer Dominick, Mrs. C. E. Potter, Harvey Fisk's birthday party, and a clambake and dance by Thomas Lamont. The Shaw Girls were a popular singing group performing there. They once entertained a party of more than 300 people.

Mary Louise Dodge fondly remembers the ice cream cones — one scoop for a nickel and two scoops for a dime. Ken Schenck remembered the good food, especially the lobster dinners. He said that whenever he wanted a snack, he could always manage to get something tasty there.

Mrs. Lee sold the place to Andrew Carson in 1919, who sold it in 1925 to John Gay, and then it was sold to Knowles Smith of Montauk. Coincidentally, the death of Mrs. Lee on January 15, 1928, was also the end of the Pavilion. It burned to the ground within a day of her death.

At the Head of the Harbor was a favorite spot along Three Mile Harbor Road. The **Three Mile Harbor Inn, Restaurant, and Cottages,** was opened in 1941 by Joe and Margaret Ambrose. They sold it in 1978

to the Loris twins, Kevin and Coco, and their sister, Barbara. In 1998, it was sold and renamed **Joneen's.** George Nicholas bought the property in 2003, renaming it **3 Mile Harbor Restaurant** and **3 Mile Harbor Cottages.**

The first restaurant at Duck Creek was **The Silver Seahorse,** built in 1946 by Florence Sage Palmer. Since then, this restaurant overlooking Maidstone Harbor Marina has been named: **The Sea Wolf, Little Rock Yacht Club, Bostwicks,** and, currently, **Riccardo's,** operated by Riccardo Traslavina.

Just south of the Duck Creek area, Dick Sage, Florence Palmer's son, built his restaurant in the 1980s, calling it **The Lighthouse at Maidstone Village.** He incorporated a 5.5-meter sloop, class C, named *Jade* inside a cupola of the restaurant. Successive owners renamed it **Wings Point.** It is currently called **East Hampton Point Restaurant.**

At the foot of Gann Road, opposite the Commercial Dock, is a dockside restaurant at the Harbor Marina called **Bostwick's Seafood Grill & Oyster Bar,** named after a tenant farmer who lived on the northwestern side of Gardiner's Island where Bostwick's Point, Forest, and Bay are located. The marina's restaurant has operated under various names since its opening in 1964. The first was **The Wheelhouse,** followed by **Rumm's, Georgette's, Little Rock Lobster, Margaret's, Breakwaters,** and **East Coast Oyster Bar & Grill.** The current Bostwick's restaurant, operated by Chris Eggert and Kevin Boles, is especially popular in the evening, with its sunset view of the Harbor and Sammy's Beach.

Above: 1970s advertisement for The Silver Seahorse
Facing Page
Top: *Lee's Pavilion, early 1900s, was the first restaurant on Three Mile Harbor. (Courtesy of the Carleton Kelsey Collection)*
Bottom, Left: *Diners enjoying the picturesque view from The Silver Seahorse (Photo found in an old newspaper advertisement)*
Bottom, Right: *1980s advertisement for The Lighthouse at Maidstone Village*

Top: *Michael's Restaurant, formerly the Fat Flounder, was originally the Hodder Poultry store in the thirties. (Photo by Diane C. Hewett)*
Middle: *Jungle Pete's on Fort Pond Boulevard, renamed Wolfies in 1988 (Photo courtesy of Vincent and Clorinda Wolfe)*
Bottom: *The Drifters performing at the Wheelhouse (now Bostwick's) in the 1960s The group from right to left: Pat Field, Harvey Field (Pat's father), name unknown, and Bill King. (Photo courtesy of Patricia Field)*

Michael's Restaurant is near Maidstone Park. It was the **Fat Flounder** in the seventies, a pizza parlor run by Gus Diamandis in 1958; a general store from 1943 to 1958 run by Raymond Tilley, his wife Diddy, son John, and partner William Widerman; and before 1943, the **Hodder Poultry Store.** Obediah Hodder, who originally came from Nova Scotia, lived here with his wife.

John Tilley recalled working in the store/deli/soda fountain, serving candy and ice cream to the young folks and beer for the grownups. After softball games at Maidstone Park, families would come in for a treat and do some socializing before heading home. There were eight booths and a jukebox to play music for dancing. There weren't many people living around there year-round in the forties, according to John. There were only two other neighborhood children, Betty Rosetti and Dave Cheney.

Jungle Pete's, a favorite night spot on Fort Pond Boulevard, was legally named **Jungle Inn** because the forested area around it looked like a jungle. Christmas tree lights were lit outside the inn all year long. Pete Federico and his wife, Nina, had square dances on Saturday nights there until the 1940s, after which the band played more modern music. Vinnie Wolf bought the place in 1972 with

Tom Collins and called it **Vinnie's Place.** In 1974, ownership changed several times and was variously called **Boatswain's, Frigate, The Birches,** and **Harry's Hideaway.** Eventually, it was bought by the Brett Corporation and was operated as **Wolfie's** by Vincent Wolf. In 1998, Paul Campanela took over the operation, keeping the name of Wolfie's.

There are also delicatessens along Three Mile Harbor Road that are also breakfast and lunch stops for many people. **Damark's,** just south of the Harbor, has provided breakfast and lunch since 1949. It has served many a "Bonac Burger" (peanut butter and butter on a hard roll). The other deli is just north of Fort Pond Boulevard. Called **The Maidstone Market,** it is a favorite stop before going to the beach at Maidstone Park or off to work. 🍃

Left: Waiting for their tables at Bostwick's Seafood Grill and Oyster Bar and enjoying the fresh air and sunset (Photo by Diane C. Hewett)
Right: An old poster for jazz at Little Rock Lobster (now Bostwick's)

Boating in the Harbor

"*There is nothing — absolutely nothing — half so much worth doing as simply messing about in boats … or with boats…. In or out of 'em, it doesn't matter."*

—*Kenneth Graham,* Wind in the Willows

Above: *The* Maidstone, *a 60-foot party boat chartered by Captain Washington Tyson Dominy (Photo courtesy of East Hampton Historical Society)*
Facing Page: *Nat Herreshoff designed and built this sloop for Charles Dana Gibson in 1896. It was brought down to Three Mile Harbor from Bar Harbor, Maine, by Linc Jewett in 1968. The sloop, named* Jilt, *was photographed by Robert H. Jewett.*

Pleasure boating became a popular pastime in Three Mile Harbor early in the twentieth century. In 1903, the Pavilion, owned by Ulysses Lee and Austin H. Culver, advertised rentals of sailboats, powerboats, and rowboats on a weekly or seasonal basis.

Ernest Miller brought the first engine-run boat here in 1902. It was a "one-lunger Lathrop." When motors expanded the usage and traveling distance for boats, boating became even more active in the Harbor.

In 1906, the naturalist John Burroughs, along with his family and guests, arrived on their 30-foot boat from West Park on the Hudson to visit Mrs. W. R. Mackay in East Hampton. The family continued these annual trips, and his son Julian eventually summered in Wainscott.

Captain W. Tyson Dominy had a 60-foot party boat, the *Maidstone*, which made excursions between Three Mile Harbor and Greenport in the 1920s. It was a fan-tail (round stern) boat, and Captain Dominy had the habit of tying the anchor line to the stern instead of to the bow, just the opposite of the norm.

Chartering parties were enjoyed both on Captain Dominy's *Maidstone* and Captain John Hussey's *A.V.H.* Their excursions were extremely popular because Captain Hussey always had interesting stories to tell about his life on the China coast. Captain Hussey also sailed on his *Emma and Lorenzo,* named after his friends Emma and Lorenzo Woodhouse.

Sailboats of all sizes were seen in the Harbor. The *Shadow*, built in 1916, was a rumrunner formerly owned by John Erickson and Harry Conklin. Edward M. Osborne, Harry's son-in-law, loved sailing on the 50-foot Herreshoff *Shadow,* which drew only 3 feet. Ed also had a sailboat that he called *Nor'easter*. He was the organizer of Snipe Races in Three Mile Harbor, held at Halsey's Marina almost every Sunday afternoon in the summer. The Snipes were five small sailboats built in Greenport, all to the same specifications. Races were held between Ed Osborne, Isaac Halsey, Edward (Olaf) Johanson, Darryl Parsons, and Ed Fitzgerald. Trophies attest to the competition between the *Emmy*, owned by Halsey, and the *Blue Shadow*, owned by Ed Osborne. In four races between 1938 and 1941, two races were won by each of them. Sherrill

Above: *Snipes on shore at Halseys'
Marina with John Custis Lawrence, the
Commodore of the Maidstone Boat
Club on the right, wearing a captain's
hat, and on the left, A. Victor Amman
(Photo courtesy of Sherrill Foster)*
Middle, Right: *Snipes racing in
Three Mile Harbor (Photo courtesy
of Donald Halsey)*
Middle, Left: *Sherrill (Nettie) Foster
with snipe race trophies
The winners listed on the large trophy:
1938 — Ike Halsey and son Donald
sailing the* Emmy; *1939 — Edward
M. Osborne and Harry Lilywhite
sailing the* Blue Shadow; *1940 —
Ike Halsey and Nettie Sherrill sailing
the* Emmy; *1941 — Edward M.
Osborne and Edward Johanson sailing
the* Blue Shadow.
*The small silver bowl trophy Sherrill
Foster holds was given to her in 1939
from the East Hampton Snipe Club for
the "Best Lady Skipper." (Photo taken
in 2000 by Sylvia Mendelman)*
Bottom: *"Amphicar" driven by Albert
Royce, Jr. (Photo courtesy of* The East
Hampton Star)*

(Nettie) Foster won a silver bowl in 1939 for "Best
Lady Skipper," and she sailed with Ike Halsey on
the *Emmy*, winning the race in 1940.

Eunice Juckett Meeker remembered "The Four
O'Clock Club" at Three Mile Harbor. After work,
the local business people would gather for sailboat
races. Nat Smith was a car repair man, so he called
his boat *Tail Light*. The camaraderie and fun were
long remembered.

Nelson Osborne had a bed-boat called the
Mishawan. This 48-footer, which made long
cruises, was captained by Billy Hand.

The "Amphicar" made headlines in July 1962.
Albert Royce, Jr., drove his convertible into the

water at the launching ramp by the Head of the
Harbor and propelled it through the water to the
Shagwong Marina, burning only 1.5 gallons of
gas an hour. Twin props and a four-cylinder engine
brought it up to a speed of 10 knots in the water.
On land, top speed attained was 70 miles per hour,
and it burned one gallon per 30 miles. Mr. Royce
was distributing this unusual vehicle for his company, Coastal Cars Company of Rutherford, New
Jersey. The price tag was $3,395.

The East Hampton Chamber of Commerce sponsored the first annual East Hampton Hydroplane
Regatta on September 23, 1962. Richard Herrlin
was the committee chairman for the race, which
involved 35 boats and the Metropolitan Inboard

Racing Association. Festivities for more than 100 people followed at the Wheelhouse Restaurant on Gann Road.

In June 1965, the Off Soundings Club brought 185 boats into Three Mile Harbor to end the first day of a two-day race. Their race began in New London, Connecticut, and ended in Shelter Island after the second day.

The Hampton Sailing Club, whose commodore was Everett T. Rattray, organized its first East End Sunfish Sailing Regatta on Sunday, August 29, 1965. Boats were launched from the south side of Sammy's Beach. The Penguin Fleet of the Hampton Sailing Club also held races. Avid sailors were Cappy Amundsen, Carl Ruff, Marvin Kuhn, Sam Robins, and Everett Rattray.

The Hampton Sailing Club held its Firecracker Bowl Regatta on July 2, 1966, with racing for its Penguin and Sunfish classes, followed by a cookout at Sammy's Beach. The chairman of the event was Eugene E. Lester, Jr.

The East Hampton Yacht Club had its headquarters at the Harbor Marina in 1966 and then moved to Wings Point (East Hampton Point), where it was quite an active organization. Other clubs joined in its annual "Chowder Bowl" regattas. Commodores and members included, among others, Seymour Kaback, Dick Sage, Fred Tobey, Peter Firis, Norman Mercer, and Michael Azarian. Membership declined in the nineties, and the group eventually disbanded.

Some boats are on land, blocked up, and holding history in their holds. There is a pintail boat at the Harbor Marina's storage yard that Fanny Gardiner remembers seeing get swamped by the waves in Gardiner's Bay while Bill Mairs and Isabel (Fanny's sister) were in the boat. This World War I torpedo retriever was built by the Bliss Co. in Greenport. Thaddeus "Babe" Osborne bought it and called it *Skippy*. It was then sold to Isabel Gardiner Mairs and afterwards, to Bob Story, who tore out its cabin and repowered it. George Rosen acquired it next and called it *Splinter*. Ralph George finally laid it to

rest in the Harbor Marina Boatyard, and it has been there ever since, its hull sheltered by trees and vines.

The *Rey Del* was a lobster boat built in Three Mile Harbor in 1938 by Harry Wessberg. It was 40 feet long, 12 feet wide, and held 2,500 pounds of lobsters in the well. The original owner, Emerson Taber, worked the boat for years from Gardiner's Bay to the Atlantic Ocean before he sold it. Reginald (Cherry) Conrad bought it years later and fixed it

up in the yard at the Harbor Marina. "I was very proud when at the helm," recalled Reg. The last known owners were from East Moriches.

If a boat can't fit into the Harbor, it anchors outside in Gardiner's Bay. In 1997, the *Itaska*, a beautifully renovated seagoing tug owned by William E. Simon, was moored for about a month just outside the mouth of the Harbor—its 150 feet impressing quite a few people here.

Above: *The* Able Hand *in 1976 (Photo courtesy of Norman J. Mercer)*

Georgica Pond Cat boats were popular here. Edwin Sherrill, Jr., kept them in repair for their owners from 1984 to 1996, but he is currently leaving the repairs to boatyards in the area.

The *Able Hand*, a 39-foot Elco built in 1929 for the honeymoon of Colonel Charles and Anne Morrow Lindbergh, participated in a Connecticut Bicentennial celebration in 1976. The ship paraded down the Mystic River with other antique and classic boats, winning the "Small Ships Best Overall" award. The proud owner, Norman J. Mercer of East Hampton, also paraded her in the New York City boat parade on the Hudson River on July 4, 1978, joining the tall ships as they sailed by the Statue of Liberty. He then bought a 39-foot Columbia, built in 1971, and named it *Sea Carol*, for his wife, Carol. He remains an avid sailor today.

The East End Classic Boat Society held its first festival in September 1998 at Gardiner's Marina, involving one-of-a-kind vessels with time-proven design and excellent craftsmanship. The diversity of boats was evident in antique canoes, sailboats, and work boats. There was a good collection of old wooden boats, among them the *Lisa Ann*, a 35-foot gaff-rigged sailboat designed by Colin Archer and built by The Freepoint Boat Builders in 1935. The owner, Captain Scannella, loved her as soon as he saw her.

Ray Hartjen displayed his Swedish sloop *Siskiwit*, built in 1948 by Jac Iverson and brought over to the Great Lakes by Dr. Pierpoint for racing in Lake Superior. The boat was also displayed at the Annapolis Boat Show, and it has been in Three Mile Harbor since 1994.

Other boats in the festival were the L. Francis Herreshoff ketch named *Quiet Tune*, a Murray Peterson schooner, a converted lobster boat, a converted Navy lifeboat yacht, a 48-foot L. Francis Herreshoff, and a 12-foot varnished lapstrake sharpie.

Representing the bass boats were a Friendship sloop, a 1915 William Hand V-bottom launch, a Connecticut River drag boat, a 1916 Crosby catboat, a MacKensie Cuttyhunk, a Brunnell, a Crosby Striper, and a Bob Dolly.

Dick Williams enjoys sailing his *Prince of Wales*, a 12-foot replica of the America's Cup winner. Twelve-meter sloops have raced in the America's Cup for twenty years. This boat can carry a skipper of up to 250 pounds, who steers with his feet. Sailing characteristics are similar to the full-sized boat and can point quite high —15 degrees. The replica was built in the 1980s, but these "Illusions" are no longer being made.

In 1998, the boat that stole the show in Three Mile Harbor was an 85-foot sailboat named *Sirocco*, owned by Mort Schrader. People would stop to admire its beauty as it made its way through the Harbor. Other boats that impressed onlookers at Three Mile Harbor were Billy Joel's *Islander/Redhead*, William C. Ford's *Sea Lion*, Pierre Pasteur's *Crazy Horse* catamaran, Norman Mercer's *Sea Carol*, and George Wilson's red-sailed *Aliento*. The Millennium brought the 85-foot luxury yacht *Eastern Star* into the Harbor. She chartered cruises out of Gardiner's Marina.

A Chinese junk sailed into the Harbor in the 1970s and stayed at Halsey's Marina. Rumors bandied about that its hold was filled with Chinese treasures from "Ripley's Believe it or Not." The advertising executive who owned her later had it docked in New York City.

The great variety of boats in Three Mile Harbor — the commercial fishing boat, small skiff, pleasure boat, cruiser, sport boat, sharpie, rowboat, kayak, canoe, ski boat, yacht, and sunfish — make the Harbor both fascinating and feasible for all! ⚓

Above: *Ship's Wheel with reflections of Gardiner's Marina (Photo by Diane C. Hewett)*
Left: *Richard Williams's* Prince of Wales, *a 12-foot replica of the 12-meter sloops raced in the America's Cup (Photo by Sylvia Mendelman)*

Looking Ahead

*T*here are many memories of Three Mile Harbor still silent, some never to be told. Perhaps this book will spark some of those memories and enrich the lives of future generations. Let us hope that this gem of East Hampton will keep its sparkle and be treasured by all. It has made a connection to the hearts of the people who have come to know it — and to the whole world.

Dr. Arthur Terry, of East Hampton, decided to physically show Three Mile Harbor's connection to the world by having its geographic position painted on the road at the Head of the Harbor. The Highway Department painted a circle with two dissecting lines, one for 41 degrees north latitude and the other for 72 degrees 11 minutes west longitude. On my globe at home, I found this 41st parallel and followed its linear connection around the world. It crossed the Atlantic Ocean, touching land again at Porto, Portugal. It traveled on to Salamanca in Spain, the northern tip of Sardinia, just north of Naples, and then spanned the Adriatic Sea. It traversed Albania, touched the southern tip of Macedonia, crossed Greece, and pierced the heart of Istanbul. It climbed the Caucasian Mountains in Armenia and Azerbaijan before crossing the Caspian Sea. Cities with hard-to-pronounce names, like Namangan in Uzbekistan and Hongliuyuan and Zhangjiakou in China, were touched. After crossing North Korea, it entered the Sea of Japan, touching the northern tip of the Island of Honshu, Japan, before setting out across the mighty Pacific Ocean. It spanned the United States, touched Eureka, California; Humboldt, Nevada; the Great Salt Lake in Utah; Cheyenne, Wyoming; Omaha, Nebraska; Ft. Wayne, Indiana; Stroudsburg, Pennsylvania; Greenwich, Connecticut; Cutchogue, New York, and finally East Hampton, Long Island.

The 2002 Winter Olympics, an event bringing together athletes from around the world, took place on this 41st parallel in Salt Lake City, Utah. Knowing that we have something in common with people around the world, perhaps the caring attitudes that we show for our treasure here in East Hampton will have a ripple effect, inspiring people to preserve the world's resources.

The preservation of the Harbor's waters for the future is of utmost concern to our Town, especially to those who live around the Harbor. Many groups are dedicated to this endeavor, and we hope their efforts will help keep this cerulean gem of East Hampton sparkling to ensure the enjoyment of Three Mile Harbor for all for years to come.

Above, top: *The old light at the entrance to Three Mile Harbor silhouetted at sunset (Photo by Randy Handwerger)*
Above, bottom: *The 41st parallel north latitude marked at the Head of the Harbor, September 7, 1961 (Photo courtesy of* The East Hampton Star)

Margaret Ambrose, proprietor of Three Mile Harbor Inn

Stanley Becker, a former owner and boater at Halsey's Marina

Peter Bistrian, local resident and businessman

Fanny Gardiner Collins, daughter of Winthrop Gardiner

Reginald Conrad, born 1913, boat owner

Bunny Cox, former operator of Cox's Fishing Station

Grace Cunkle, resident of Springs

Diane Dayton, assistant, East Hampton Library

Rudy DeSanti, Sr., developer of Woodbine Drive

Mary Louise Dodge, born 1915, still lives in house on Springs Fireplace where she was born

Betty Dragotta, wife of developer, Augie, the brother-in-law of Rudi DeSanti, Sr.

Anthony Drexel Duke, founder of Boys Harbor

Helen Palmer Edwards, wife of James Edwards and daughter of Steve Palmer

Louis Edwards (son of Charles), wife Marion, and daughter Harriet

Norma Edwards (cousin of Mary Louise Dodge)

Abigail Edwards Field (daughter of Daniel Edwards), born April 15, 1898

Sherrill Foster, local historian and journalist

Robert David Lion Gardiner, 16th Lord of the Manor

Ralph George, born 1929, former Marine patrolman

Alexandra Goelet, daughter of Alexandra Gardiner Creel

Ray Hartjen, local educator, writer, owner of Siskiwit sloop

Richard Herrlin, homeowner on the eastern shore in the house formerly owned by I.Y. Halsey

Estelle Hulse, resident, now deceased

Olive King Jewett (daughter of George and Agnes King), wife of Link Jewett, residents

Robert Jewett and wife, Betty, residents

Carleton Kelsey, born 1913, Amagansett librarian and historian

Trevor Kelsol, East Hampton Village historian

Dorothy King, East Hampton Library's historian

Clarence E. King and wife, Emma Mae (daughter of Florus Miller), residents

Hugh King, East Hampton historian and "Town Crier"

Gayle Lester, wife of Fred Lester of Round Swamp Farm

Josephine Little, wife of John Little, now deceased

Susan Miller McCarthy, resident

Don MacKay, Captain of the Captain Kidd

Isabele Mairs, daughter of Winthrop Gardiner

Eunice Juckett Meeker, local journalist, now deceased

Norman Mercer, resident artist and sailor

Milton Miller, bayman, lived in Olympic Heights

Edward Monroe Osborne, born 1905, now deceased, and wife, Ethel Diffene Osborne

Fred Overton, East Hampton Town Clerk and clam chowder expert

Larry Penny, Director of the East Hampton Town Natural Resources Department

Elizabeth Crawford Porrior, native plants landscaper

William Petrat, relative of Jim Taylor

James Quackenbush, resident of Three Mile Harbor

Kennell Schenck, resident of East Hampton Village, now deceased

Mary Ann Siegfried, Springs Historical Society

Carolyn Lester Snyder (daughter of Albert Cullum Lester and Barbara Grace Lester), of Round Swamp Farm

Jim Taber, son of Emerson Taber

Aileen Talmage (wife of Richard Talmage, now deceased), resident of Springs

John Tilley, son of Raymond and Gertrude ("Diddy") Tilley

Carrie Tillinghast, born 1899, wife of Edward Tillinghast, resident

Stewart Vorphal, bayman and town historian

John Warren, born 1915, worked at boatyards in Three Mile Harbor, now deceased

Richard A. Williams, resident of Three Mile Harbor

Rindi Wolf, wife of Vinnie Wolf, proprietors of Wolfie's

Vernon Jarvis Wood, born 1915, fisherman

Many heartfelt thanks to all the people who contributed to this local history. This is just a partial list of the many people who have assisted me. Unfortunately, many are no longer living, and I feel honored and privileged to have known them and to have listened to their memories.

It has been extremely rewarding to have lived here and come to know so many people who also share a heart-felt love of Three Mile Harbor.

—Sylvia Mendelman

Anderson, Robert Charles, *The Great Migration Begins*, Vol. II (1620–1633 to New England), 1995, New England Historical Genealogy Society, Boston, MA

Bailey, Paul, *Long Island*, Vol.1, 1949, Suffolk County Historical Association, Riverhead, NY

Book Hampton, Inc., and Jorge Gentilini, *East Hampton from Wainscott to Montauk*, 1973, Bookhampton Inc., East Hampton, NY

Clark, Beth, *Ann Hutchinson*, 1967, © 2000 Chelsea House Publishers, Philadelphia, PA

Connecticut Society of Genealogists, Inc., *The Connecticut Nutmegger*, Vol. 29, No.4, 1997, Glastonbury, CT

Cooper, Thomas, *The Records of the Court of Sessions of Suffolk County in the Province of New York, 1670–1688*, 1993, Suffolk County, NY

Daniels, Norton W. (Bucket), *My East Hampton*, 1991, East Hampton, NY

Dan's Papers, *Our Hampton Heritage*, Vol. II, 1984, Dan's Papers, Bridgehampton, NY

Denton, Daniel, "Brief Description of New York, 1670," from the *Historic Chronicles of New Amsterdam*, 1845, West Gowans, NY

East Hampton Chamber of Commerce, *Long Island's East Hampton Area*, 1971, East Hampton, NY

East Hampton Town Records

East Hampton Trustees Records

Edwards, J. S., *History of John Edwards Family*, 1899, San Leandro, CA

Edwards, Thomas M., *Reminiscences of Old East Hampton by the Sea*, 1929, East Hampton Library, East Hampton, NY

En Plein Air — The Art Colonies of East Hampton and Old Lyme, 1880–1930, Guild Hall, East Hampton, and the Florence Griswold Museum, Old Lyme, CT

Epstein & Barlow, *East Hampton: A History and Guide*, 1975, Medway Press, Wainscott, NY

Failey, Dean, *Long Island Is My Nation*, 1976, Society for Preservation of Long Island Antiquities, NY

Flint, *Early Long Island*, 1896, G. P. Putnam's Sons, NY, NY

Gardiner, David, *Chronicles of the Town of East Hampton, County of Suffolk, New York*, Copyright 1973 by Isabel Gardiner Mairs, East Hampton, NY

Gardiner, Sarah Diodati, *Early Memories of Gardiner's Island*, 1947, East Hampton Star Publications, East Hampton, NY

Gardner, Jo Ann, *Herbs in Bloom*, 1998, Timber Press, Portland, OR

Geus, Averill Dayton, *From Sea to Sea*, 1999, Phoenix Publications, Kennebunk, ME

Geus, Averill Dayton, *Fifty Years of the Maidstone Club, 1941–1991*, 1991, Phoenix Publications, Kennebunk, ME

Gregory, Brenda, *The Pleasures of Herb Gardening*, 1984, Garden of Herbs, Wainscott, NY

Halsey, William Donaldson, *Sketches from Local History*, 1966, Bridgehampton, NY

Harpers Magazine, *A New England Colony in New York*, August 1885, NY, NY

Hedges, Henry P., *A History of East Hampton*, 1897, J. H. Hunt, Sag Harbor, NY

Hedges, Henry P., *Historic East Hampton*, 1899, East Hampton Library, East Hampton, NY

Holden, Albert, *A Pictorial History of Montauk*, II edition, 1983, Holden's Publications, Montauk, NY

Hummel, Charles, *With Hammer In Hand*, 1968, Winterthur Museum, Delaware, Museum University
        Press of Virginia, Charlottsville, VA

Lester, John, *Memoirs and Forebears*, 1998, East Hampton, NY

Lewis, Alanzo, and James R. Newhall, *History of Lynn, Essex County, Massachusetts*, 1865, John L.
        Shorey, Boston, MA. Reprinted in 1989 by Heritage Books, Bowie, MD

MacKay, Robert, and Richard Welch, *Long Island: An Illustrated History*, Society for the Preservation
        of Long Island Antiquities, 2000, American Historical Press, Sun Valley, CA

Martin, John Frederick, *Profits In The Wilderness*, 1991, University of North Carolina Press,
        Chapel Hill, NC

Matthiessen, Peter, *Men's Lives*, 1986, Random House, NY, NY

Miller, George Sid, "Springs or Accabonac" in Chamber of Commerce's *300 Years in East Hampton*,
        East Hampton, NY

New York State Archaeological Association Indian Museum, Southold, NY

O'Sullivan, Ilse, *East Hampton and the American Revolution*, 1976, East Hampton Town Bicentennial
        Committee, East Hampton, NY

Payne, Robert, *The Island*, 1959, Harcourt, Brace & Co., NY, NY

Rattray, Everett T., *The South Fork*, 1979, Random House, NY, NY

Rattray, Jeannette Edwards, *East Hampton History Including Genealogies*, 1953, East Hampton, NY, NY

Rattray, Jeannette Edwards, *Ship Ashore 1610-1955*, 1955, Coward McCann Inc., NY, NY

Rattray, Jeannette Edwards, *Three Centuries in East Hampton, Long Island, NY*, 1937,
        East Hampton Star Press, East Hampton, NY

Rattray, Jeannette Edwards, *Fifty Years of the Maidstone Club 1891-1941*, 1941, the Maidstone Club,
        East Hampton, NY

Ruther, Frederick, *Some Cogent Observations About Long Island*, 1904, © 1909, Hicksville, NY

Springs Historical Society, East Hampton, NY

Springs Improvement Society, *Springs, A Celebration*, 1984, East Hampton, NY

Stein, Donna, *Colonial East Hampton 1640-1800*, Guild Hall and East Hampton Historical Society, 1998,
        350th Anniversary Celebration of the Town of East Hampton, NY

Stone, Gaynell, *The Coastal Archaeological Readings*, Vol. 2, 1978, Suffolk County Archaeological Assn., 1978, Stonybrook, NY

Strong, John A., *The Montaukett Indians of Eastern Long Island*, 2001, Syracuse University Press, Syracuse, NY

Southampton Town 325th Anniversary Book, 1965, Southampton, NY

South Fork Natural History Society, *Gardiners Island*, Vol. 6, No. 1, 1994, Amagansett, NY

Suffolk County Archaeological Association, Vol. III, *History and Archaeology of the Montauk Indians*, 1979, Ginn Custom Publishing, Lexington, MA

Suffolk County Historical Society Register, 1975, The Society, Riverhead, NY

Suffolk County's Ten Great Townships of Long Island, 1930–40, Board of Supervisors of Suffolk County Publicity Committee, Riverhead, NY (compliments of Perry B. Duryea)

Talmage, Ferris, *The Springs*, 1970, The Steamboat Press, Southampton, NY

The East Hampton Star, East Hampton, NY

"The Great Migration Newsletter," Vol. 1, 1990, New England Historic and Genealogical Society, Boston, MA

The History Project, Inc., Tony Prohaska and East Hampton Library, The History Project, Amagansett, NY

The Independent, East Hampton, NY

The New York Times, NY, NY

Tooker, William Wallace, *The Indian Place-Names*, 1911, John Jermain Library, G.P. Putnam's Sons, NY, NY

Town of East Hampton Comprehensive Plan, 1984

Town of East Hampton Lecture Series for the 350th Anniversary Celebration of the Town of East Hampton, 1648–1998, East Hampton Library, East Hampton, NY

Vickers, Daniel, *Farmers and Fishermen* (Essex County 1630–1850), 1994, University of North Carolina Press, Chapel Hill, NC

Wick, Steven, "The First Long Islanders" from *Long Island: Our Story*, 1997, Newsday, Inc., Melville, Long Island, NY

Wood, Joseph, *The New England Village*, 1997, Johns Hopkins University Press, Baltimore, MD

Wood, Silas, *Sketch of the First Settlement of the Several Towns on Long Island*, 1824, Alden Spooner, Brooklyn, NY